# Cloud
# of
# Witnesses

# Cloud of Witnesses

Letters for the Pilgrim

Jason David Eubanks, MD

DAWN TREADER

*To my fellow pilgrims in progress....*

*When at the first I took my Pen in hand,*
*Thus for to write; I did not understand*
*That I at all should make a little Book*
*In such a mode; Nay, I had undertook*
*To make another, which when almost done,*
*Before I was aware, I this begun.*
    *And thus it was: I writing of the Way*
*And Race of Saints in this our Gospel-Day...*
*About their Journey, and the way to Glory....*

—John Bunyan

# Books by Jason David Eubanks, MD

*Book of Hours: Meditations for the Heart after God*

*Twelve Stones: Apologetics for an Age of Relativism*

*Gentlest of Ways*

*More of Him, Less of Me:*
*A Doctor's Devotional for Spiritual Health*

*For the Joy of Obeying*

*Rotations: A Medical Student's Clinical Experience*

# Contents

# Author's Note

*It's in literature that true life can be found. It's under the mask of fiction that you can tell the truth.*

—*Gao Xingjian*

Warning! What follows is a work of fiction. The reader who does not delight in imaginative leaps should best turn back. For the journey that lies ahead requires a spoonful of wonder, in addition to the usual heaping tablespoon of grace, to gulp the medicine down.

But just because the pages that follow are a work of fiction, does not mean they might not help reveal truth. Indeed, quite the contrary. For as Ralph Waldo Emerson reminds us, "Fiction reveals truth that reality obscures." Sometimes the most memorable truths emerge from beneath the mask of fiction. Spiritual truths are no exception.

In fact, when I consider my own spiritual development, some of the most foundational truths of my faith came to me as I wiggled my toes in the soil of Narnia and Middle-earth. In these fictional worlds, truth became knowable; narrative made truth relatable. For truth, as the 17th century polymath, Francis Bacon, puts it, "is so hard to tell, it sometimes needs fiction to make it plausible."

What follows, therefore, is an attempt at truth under the mask of an epistolary novel—or a novel of letters. This genre blossomed in the 18th century with the publication of Samuel Richardson's *Pamela*. The epistolary novel has survived, in various iterations, ever since. And though handwritten letters are becoming increasingly anachronistic in a world of email, text messaging and tweets, even the youth might still admit something special about a letter. For handwritten correspondence still possesses a personal and endearing quality unparalleled by its electronic competitors. There is a timelessness to epistles.

No doubt this is in part why the Lord chose to communicate so much of His truth to mankind in the timeless form of letters. Christ could have come in the 21st century, tweeting His first arrival and posting His pictures on social media. But of course, He didn't. He chose to arrive to the heralding of angels instead. He elected to begin His ministry in a world of oral tradition and handwritten letters.

Through this word of mouth and snail mail, however, Christ's gospel spread across the globe. The Good News walked into hearts on the legs of epistles which speak to us in the 21st century with as much love and power as they might have to the Galatians or the Corinthians in the 1st century. And because of the timeless quality of these epistles, I've dared to believe that even immortal angels might find reason to enjoy writing and reading a series of letters.

So the pages that follow aim to do just that: detail a journey of faith as it plays out in an angelic correspondence. The letters comprising this communication further unveil a fictional exegesis of Hebrews 11, intended to deepen and broaden our understanding of biblical faith. Through this effort, I hope to encourage the heart of every other pilgrim who is treading alongside me in this difficult—but rewarding!—journey we call the life of faith.

—J.D. Eubanks, MD

Therefore, since we are surrounded by such a great cloud of witnesses, let us throw off everything that hinders and the sin that so easily entangles, and let us run with perseverance the race marked out for us. Let us fix our eyes on Jesus, the Author and Perfecter of our faith, who for the joy set before Him endured the cross, scorning its shame, and sat down at the right hand of the throne of God. Consider Him who endured such opposition from sinful men, so that you will not grow weary and lose heart.

Hebrews 12:1-3

# Preface

Two flights of stairs paralleled the escalators connecting the bright June day to the subterranean gloom beneath a Budapest recently emerging from the Iron Curtain. We were off the train and headed to a hostel on the far side of the city. The fastest way to get there: the subway.

The weekday traffic hustled along and we simply followed down. At least that is the way it felt at the time. For although I thought it strange no one appeared to be buying tickets or showing passes, in my youthful naiveté I thought: maybe this is "public" transportation in Budapest—free? Or perhaps, that's what my student-minded budget hoped for. And the freely revolving gate arms at the tunnel's edge didn't disavow me of my illusion, until....

We were spotted by the posse of uniformed men standing in the shadows on the other side. At a minimum, our giant backpacks gave us away. We clearly weren't Budapestians. And before I knew it, the Iron Curtain opened like the gates of Hell before a pack of angry and screaming men in pursuit. Instinctually, we turned and ran.

That's when he showed up. Out of nowhere. A local Budapester who grabbed my intrepid mother by the arm, and raced with her up the stairs, while I galloped the descending escalator, retrograde. Back in the light of day, he spoke perfect English, if it weren't for all the obscenities. Every other word was "f___" this and "f___" that, especially those vigilante guards down in the subway. (I guess if you learned your English from American movies and TV—as he said he did—you *would* think every noun needed to be preceded by an expletive!) But then his coarse language was

1

balanced by his heavenly kindness. He placed us on a bus headed toward the hostel. He was gone as quickly as he arrived.

That's the way we remember the "F_____ Angel," or so we lovingly call him to this day. The foul-mouthed man, the angel I still contend, who showed up to guard and guide us just when we needed it. You may ask, "Do I believe in angels?" To which, if you mean the cherubic, canvas children of Raphael or Peter Paul Rubens, then decidedly "No!" But if by angels you mean the characters of Scripture, those radiant, awe-inspiring and powerful manifestations of God's presence, then "Yes!" I do. And further, if I'm asked, "Do you believe in guardian angels?" then again I would say without hesitation, "Yes, I do!" For Christ Himself alludes to them, and I've felt their presence numerous times. I've seen them with my own two eyes (Mt 18:10).

Contemporary Western culture seems more fascinated by the demonic, however, not Heaven's angels. There seems to be no absence of devils, ghosts and ghouls portrayed in tattoo body ink or on the movie screens. Halloween is a playful (or not so playful?) parade of these dark characters.

Amidst this sorry spectacle, Christianity has largely lost an appreciation for angelic activity. The work of angels has been pigeonholed to the pages of an ancient Bible. Their awe-inspiring presence has been emasculated in the Western mind by artistic renditions and "enlightened," philosophical argument.

But in the Far East, where the gospel is still stretching its new-found legs, angelic activity is noted with active, biblical proportions in the here and now. To read an autobiography like Brother Yun's *The Heavenly Man*, for example, is to be convinced the angels of Scripture are just what Scripture describes them to be: mighty servants of God sent to minister to those who will inherit salvation (Heb 1:14).[1]

But what does it mean that angels have been sent to serve the saved? Do angels speak the Spirit's counsel? Are they the strong arms of the Father's protection? Are angels independently minded like the men they serve? And is angelic service given

---

[1] Brother Yun, *The Heavenly Man* (Oxford, England: Lion Hudson IP Ltd., 2002).

willingly or begrudgingly? Do angels find the humans they're called to serve laughable, pitiful, maddening, or exasperating? Perhaps, in their best moments, men might be endearing or inspiring to the angels. While the answers to these questions would not change my faith, personally I think it would be fun to know (and one day we will!).

No doubt a similar kind of thinking once went through the mind of C.S. Lewis in writing *The Screwtape Letters*. In fact, in reflecting on those *Letters*—to which the current work owes a great debt—C.S. Lewis admits to a kind of inner grudge in which the demonic conversations of Uncle Screwtape and Wormwood were not balanced by a similar dialogue between an archangel and a guardian angel. For in such a dialogue, it might be possible to imagine the nature and tenor of the angelic service the writer of Hebrews alludes to.

As Lewis argued, however, the potential trouble is that such a discourse would be subject to a high bar. He said, "every sentence would need to smell of Heaven." And in Lewis' opinion, the prose of this angelic discourse would have to exceed the finest work of the mystic, Thomas Traherne—or the more popular Shakespeare, Dante, or Milton as your tastes prefer.[2]

Yet although my faith and spiritual thinking are deeply indebted to my brother in Christ, C.S. Lewis, and I agree with almost everything the Spirit worked out through his writings, on this linguistic point I humbly dare to disagree. For though I am no philologist, I am a life-long student of Scripture. And through its pages, I have come to know angels as beings who are quite capable of speaking the unornamented language of men. When they converse with Abraham, Joshua, Zechariah or Mary, they do so not in an unapproachable and lofty style, but rather in the vernacular. Though their presence instills a holy fear, they speak simply and straight. And while angels may be capable of speaking in a mellifluous, heavenly tongue, when they converse with humanity, they do so in a language all men—priests, shepherds and adolescent

---

[2] C.S. Lewis, *The Screwtape Letters* (New York: HarperCollins, 2013), xliii.

girls—might understand. In fact, by extension, they might even dare to blend in with some Budapestian expletives!

In the same vein, I am of the opinion that angelic activity on earth is *not* limited to obviously ethereal manifestations. For I believe in a God who left His throne in Heaven, took on the flesh of men, was born in a manager, and spent His years of ministry eating, laughing, weeping, and conversing with prostitutes, tax collectors, and "sinners." Before He unveiled His ministry, He spent decades cloaking majesty in humble obscurity. He defied social boundaries and eschewed religious snobbery. He chose to get His hands and feet dirty with the spiritually dirty. And if the Creator of the universe deigned to do such things, why shouldn't His servants? For as Christ said, the servant is not above his master (Mt 10:24).

So I contend that any angelic conversation (real or imagined) meant for the spiritual ears of men would not be circumscribed to exalted language, but rather the everyday exchange of men's society. It must be accessible to both the professor of literature and the beer-brawler falling asleep in her class; it must speak to the logic of the lawyer and the moral conscience of the factory worker alike. And if, as C.S. Lewis rightly suggests, such an angelic conversation must also "smell of Heaven," then this dialogue needs at the same time to be rooted in the discourse *of* Heaven: Scripture. This written word comes from the Word, and His life animates all life in Heaven and on earth—angelic, human or otherwise. When the angels speak, therefore, they speak the truth of the Word.

With these methodological considerations in tow, the larger goal of this work is an exploration and affirmation of faith. What is faith and how does it manifest in our lives? How did it evidence in the lives of those faithful witnesses who have gone before us? What can we learn from their journeys to challenge and encourage our own pilgrimages?

Pondering such questions, I invariably found myself drawn to the discussion of faith in the book of Hebrews. It seemed to me that the cloud of witnesses mentioned in the twelfth chapter, and the heroes of faith in the eleventh, might prove the perfect ground for such an examination. By extension, the cloud of witnesses then led me to consider a heavenly company; and as a result, an angelic conversation emerged as the narrative construct for the epistolary exploration of faith that follows.

It should be noted here, however, that this narrative conceit is put forth simply as a tool of fiction intended to help flesh out some of the salient principles of biblical faith. What this work does *not* intend is a definitive theological statement on the cloud of witnesses itself: Is it composed of active spectators in the heavenly realms whose prayers for the pilgrims are offered up to the throne of God by ministering angels (Rev 5:8; 8:3)? Or is this cloud of witnesses to be viewed in a more historic and static sense: As a collection of testifiers whose former lives on earth still bear witness to the power of faith and God's faithfulness? Is it potentially both? And where are these witnesses now: In Heaven, or still asleep in some intermediary place, waiting to rise with the resurrection?

To these questions, the current work makes no attempt at definitive theological conclusions. For frankly, none can be had. No matter how many letters follow behind one's name, God alone knows for sure. And the reader who may find himself theologically tripped up by the narrative conceit of this work because of some entrenched opinion, will sadly miss this book's intent: encouraging the faithful and glorifying the Author and Perfecter of faith itself—Jesus Christ our Lord.

So whatever one's thoughts might be about guardian angels, the language of the heavenly realms, or the cloud of witnesses itself, I encourage the reader to temporarily suspend opinion and join the journey ahead. With such an imaginative leap, it might prove possible to be spiritually edified and entertained at the same time. I hope to encourage your pilgrimage in this way.

Now may the words of our mouths, the meditations of our hearts, and work our lives be pleasing to Christ, the Author and Perfecter of our faith!

# The Letters

# Letter 1

Beloved Barnabas,

I've just left the company of Gabriel and Raphael, where our conversation happened to turn to you. I promised to check in and see how you're settling in on your newest mission. Have you prepared for the long haul? For as I'm sure you've already figured out, you have your work cut out for you in the pilgrim you've been assigned. He is one of those skeptical types who asks endless questions. Your efforts will constantly interface with his ceaseless—and I'm sure you'll find, sometimes exasperating!—self-dialogue. Your success will depend upon exploiting the doors his skepticism opens. See his pointed questions as opportunities!

Speaking of which, let's not miss a single teachable moment in the life of your pilgrim, and turn our attention to your labor now. For the archangels attending our Father's throne have noted with interest the recent increase in prayers from your pilgrim. Of course, the volume of these prayers is not the concern. Our Father loves His children's pleas, however pesky or pitiful they might be. And in truth, our Lord would love the pilgrim's entire life to be one long, continuous prayer.

Recently, however, both the tenor and content of your pilgrim's prayers have become disquieting. You have undoubtedly noticed how his petitions now seem filled with doubt and tinged with a certain despair. In short, your pilgrim appears to be questioning his faith.

As you know, Barnabas, this is a matter of grave importance. Not because doubt, in and of itself, is to be feared—our Lord never fears probing questions—but rather, because nurtured doubt can be that beachhead our enemy soon exploits to the ruin of our trusts. On the flipside, however, a man who does not dwell in doubt gives the devil no foothold in his faith. For the Liar knows, when a man risks faith, he risks everything. The believer says with his whole life: I am sure of what I hope for and certain of what I do not see. Therefore, our enemy devises to intervene before a man's faith is entrenched. Because when a pilgrim deeply seats his life of faith in Christ, that man becomes unmovable.

As you can attest, however, this kind of commitment is much more than a deep-seated trust. It is the infinite resignation of a love so earnest and true in its intentions that it induces a man to die with Christ that he might be united with our Lord. The man of faith dares to invest his entire being with a Source of Being he cannot see. Here lies the great challenge of faith—one which we angels may not fully understand, living as we do within the visible knowledge and security of our heavenly realms.

Indeed, on this point our enemy may actually have the upper hand, dear Barnabas. For having once walked the halls of Heaven, only to fall to his present depths, Satan intimately knows the vast differential between angelic apprehension and mortal speculation. He grasps the magnitude of man's challenge in a unique way. And armed with this understanding, the Liar will take all measures to convince the pilgrim his faith is in vain. For if this lie succeeds, then the pilgrim's entire existence breaks down. His gamble seems too great. He stands to lose his reason for being. So as I'm sure you'll agree, the utterance of such prayers from your pilgrim calls for your fullest attention and your highest vigilance!

In difficult cases like these, dear Barnabas, my time as a guardian taught me that a pilgrim's doubt is best reformed by a shift in perspective. For isn't that why he is questioning his faith in the first place? He has taken his eyes off his Pole Star.

Perhaps you have noticed how his doubt has coincided with an increasing focus on himself. When pilgrims like him begin to look to themselves, they invariably avert their gaze from Heaven. And when Christ is no longer front and center, our enemy quickly fills our

Lord's place with some competing "god" of his own. But though the sky might be full of stars, a ship navigating by anything other than True North will never reach the harbor of its hopes.

Challenging cases like these, therefore, demand timely and creative intervention: Perhaps you'll become the garrulous man on the plane who engages your pilgrim's captive audience; maybe you'll work in the reflection that comes on the heels of the near accident you help prevent; or perchance, his heart will be moved by that unexpected call you orchestrate at that most opportune time. Might you simply shock him with a momentary glimpse of your radiance? I've always found a little fear and trembling goes a long way.

The details of the specific interventions the Spirit will work out through you. But by whatever providential means necessary, the pilgrim's attention must be gained. The demon in your man must be driven out and the temple made clean to be filled with the Spirit. Though the task seems great, however, take heart: Our Lord will not lose anyone entrusted to Him!

In humbly assisting the Spirit's effort, however, I have often found it instructive to return to the basics—first things being first. Begin by reawakening the eyes of your pilgrim's faith. Draw his attention to what he cannot ignore: the beauty of the world around him. For creation holds the seeds of faith. And if you can induce your pilgrim to look intently into the majesty of God's world, sooner or later the spectacular details of this creation will move him. Indeed, I have found all but the most obdurate fools or inveterate narcissists are capable of admitting there must be a God behind it all. For ironically, the more man's scientific explorations delve into the mysteries of God's creation, the more impossible the facts make it for him to cling to the spurious belief it all comes down to chance.

But you must help keep your man's eyes wide open, Barnabas. For these pilgrims are so prone to sleep walking! Lost in the lullaby of comfort, they can waste years of possible growth in their wandering, spiritual somnambulism! So don't be afraid to douse him with a little heavenly water if needed. Wake him up!

Once you've used the beauty and majesty of the universe to help open the door of faith, then the real work ensues. For as you've no doubt observed, there is huge difference between admitting an intelligent design behind creation—their so-called "watchmaker" God—and claiming a personal, loving God as Lord of one's life. For the former admission requires no real commitment. But the latter necessitates an ongoing relationship: stratified with God above and man below, and bound by the requisite daily

13

sacrifices of faith. And perhaps understandably, these concessions are not easily offered. They always make a demand on the man.

In this labor of love, therefore, it is of utmost importance to remind your pilgrim he is not alone. For it seems a sense of isolation, much like fatigue, can serve as one of our enemy's greatest tools in diverting faithful souls onto the broad and populous roads leading to destruction. Once on those crowded causeways, however, it becomes increasingly difficult to extract your man from the crowd.

To keep him on the straight and narrow, therefore, your pilgrim must then be made to recall the great cloud of witnesses who have preceded him. He must be drawn to consider all those saints who—like our angelic host—watch and pray over him. He must see that he is never truly alone. For not only has our Lord promised to never leave him or forsake him, but the Father has also added to His triune singularity all those faithful lives who attest to the glory, goodness and majesty of our King. In the frailty and imperfection of their earthly lives, these saints are often the pilgrims' best teachers. Your man may find in their lives points of identification which encourage his foundering faith.

To the topics I have just described, the Spirit inspired that holy letter to the Hebrews in which He discusses faith with a two-pronged attack: First by drawing man's attention to the beauty of the created world; and then, by shifting His focus to those memorable saints of the faith (culminating with Christ Himself) whose lives demonstrate God's glory. Your work will be best served, therefore, by bringing your pilgrim's attention to this text; and by some means, causing him to carefully consider the examples therein. For a life of faith without those shining stars must seem like an ocean too broad to cross.

But our Lord's infinite wisdom anticipated this trepidation. So in His Word, God has given His children the account of one life after another that stepped toward Him in faith. If you can convince your pilgrim to focus on those footsteps, he might be enticed to keep his course. He might have the courage to see that no ocean is too broad or deep to cross for those who are strengthened by God's love to persevere in faith.

So in the peculiar words of our mortal cousins, dear Barnabas, "put your shoulder to the wheel." Make haste to attend to the details we've discussed. Be a son of encouragement to your weary pilgrim. In so doing, I'm confident that He who began a good work in you will carry it through to completion!

Affectionately yours,
## Uriel

# Letter 2

Beloved Barnabas,

Your response to my recent letter has impressed upon me the urgency of our current concerns. It seems our sense of your pilgrim's doubt is well founded. His current predicament reminds me of the professor I was once charged with. That man was a handful before the Spirit finally corralled him! The professor had a retort for each suggestion and a riposte for every argument. His doubt was a trembling mountain that had to come crumbling down before we could rebuild on the sure foundation.

Your man is in a comparatively better spot. Nonetheless, because of his wavering belief, my last correspondence referenced that letter to the Hebrews and its two-pronged discourse on faith. As I pointed out, this discussion begins by linking the unseen power of faith with the undeniable beauty and majesty of God's created world. For while faith deals with the invisible, all that is visible comes from and points to the infinite Invisibility behind all things. Faith is the link from the seen to the unseen.

Perhaps no attribute of the visible world more fully reveals the unseen qualities of our Lord than beauty. For as you and I know well,

Barnabas, beauty dwells with the Lord. As our cousin David sings, the blessed love to gaze upon the beauty of our King. (But really, how could they not! For have you and I not also been transfixed by His beauty? It is spellbinding!)

This same beauty of our Lord has overflowed like a fountain into the details of His created world. Creation is awash in its splendor. Forgetting all other arguments, proofs or reasons for men to believe in God, this beauty singlehandedly undermines the atheists' strongest attacks.

But we must give credit where credit is due and fully acknowledge the following: The biologists have cleverly described the workings of the smallest cells; the physicists have detailed the forces of the observable universe; and the biochemists have modeled the structures of life's most complex proteins. Even so, when science attempts to nullify God in this sea of revealed processes, the elegant equations emerging from these explorations cannot explain beauty. Indeed, the equations themselves are beautiful! The complex mathematics simply heighten the wonder underpinning all that men see.

So whether it is the aesthetic sense beauty arouses or the intellectual awe the universe's equations inspire, the human mind cannot ignore the wonder stitched into God's creation. Both sense and intellect intuit the presence of a divine Intelligence behind all things. For as the honest will admit: the details are simply too marvelous to be coincidental! The ineffable beauty men observe is too breathtaking to be random meaninglessness.

For though the brilliant colors of a bird might give it some survival edge, are they not also meant to bring men delight? Does the painted glory of a distant nebulae give the mindless, swirling gases what they call a "Darwinian" advantage? Must a sunset's colors move the heart to tears? Why would the heavens be awe-inspiring, unless they were meant to be so? Unless, some infinite Intelligence designed them to this end, for some specific purpose.

Now to be sure—as your savvy pilgrim might point out—some of the most stalwart atheists will nonetheless cling to their godless dogma to the very end. There seems to be no limit to their hardheadedness! Goaded by the devil, they will insist creation's wonders are the products of the random grace of chance. Can you imagine? What complete balderdash!

When your pilgrim raises such ridiculous objections, however, you must patiently reveal to him the absurdity of this line of reasoning. For ironically, the theories these atheists hide behind are undermined by the very mathematics they trust in. That is, the compound probabilities required to actualize their beliefs make their arguments nothing but statistical nonsense. Or, to use their own inflated terms, statistical de minimis.

But for the sake of argument here, even if these numeric absurdities did evolve over the millennia to produce the complex, biologic functionality men observe, the question still remains: Why is it not only functional, but beautiful? And why does beauty exist at all? Why do men like your pilgrim have the capacity to appreciate it and long for it? Why does it speak to the heart?

At this point, you might do well to remind your pilgrim of his most recent stroll through the museum of art; or cause him to reflect on his favorite piece of orchestral music. Draw his attention to the skyscraper that pierces the clouds, or the suspension bridge that spans the bay.

Does the painting not have an artist? What hands chiseled the statue's stone? Didn't the composer compile the notes of the symphony? Why is the bridge not only functional, but majestic? With this tact, sooner or later, your pilgrim will be forced to admit: there is a mind behind all artistic, created beauty. And by extension, he might then be inclined to concede the beauty in creation that moves him to tears must come, not from the carelessness of atomic chance, but rather the intentional love of a creative Intelligence beyond his comprehension.

With this line of reasoning, your pilgrim might then be induced to reflect on what the angels have long observed—how the mind of man is but a poor reflection of the Intelligence that created him. But in his finite creations, man's mind nonetheless dimly reflects the creative genius of our Father. And when a man is forced to admit this observation, he is then compelled to consider two relations: The link between Heaven and earth; and at the same time, the great distance between his own limited abilities and the undeniable intelligence he observes in the universe around him. For is this unfathomable genius an intelligence man himself can claim? Can he create the heavens?

Now unless your pilgrim is a madman lost in his own delusion, he will go with you this far. That is, he will reluctantly admit there is some kind of "intelligent" design in the universe—and one that is beyond his own. He will come as far as what they have called the "Deist" position. But to go the next step—the step of faith—requires infinitely more. It demands his whole life. And that is where we watch most pilgrims stumble.

The door of faith may be opened by the glory of the heavens and the beauty of the natural world. But as I have previously mentioned, the faith that then leads seekers to go on walking the narrow road to Heaven demands so much more. It requires the often terrifying, and temporally unrequited, sacrifices of daily life. So only the heroes, supported and sustained by the Son's grace, can make this journey of faith. Hence, the catalogue of faithful servants in God's letter to the Hebrews. More on this point later.

For the time being, however, this is where we will have to leave it, Barnabas. My attention is currently being called away by our dear brother, Haniel. As you know, he only calls when it's urgent! But when I am able, I will return to this discussion. For expounding the next point—that is, the lives of the faithful who have preceded your man—is really the crucial balm for your struggling pilgrim. Indeed, the most powerful encouragement you can provide him lies in the examples their lives of faith have set. Till then, my brother, persist in the grace of our Lord.

Affectionately yours,
*Uriel*

# Letter 3

Beloved Barnabas,

I hope it goes without saying: my heart is with you in your work. For how precious in the sight of our Father are the feet of those who labor for the Kingdom. By the report you've recently provided, I'm convinced you are doing just that—faithfully serving our King. May His grace fill you!

Now as to those labors...I described in my former letter how the beauty and majesty of God's creation allow for the possibility and plausibility of faith. But once this faith buds, only the Spirit can make it grow. And He does so by encouraging, supporting and strengthening faith through a variety of means.

One of the Spirit's many tools in this effort is the cloud of witnesses who have preceded your pilgrim. Their lives of faith speak volumes. For this reason, the epistle to the Hebrews goes on to detail the journeys of God's foremost saints. Having now overheard your pilgrim's most recent prayers, I am all the more fully convinced this text holds a treasure for your taking: a rich hoard to fund your current Kingdom work.

Recollect if you will, Barnabas, how the writer of that illustrious letter begins his discussion on the lives of faith with Abel. He is the second son of that first couple, and remembered as a righteous man whose faith still speaks, even though he is now dead to the world, but alive with us in Christ.

But why was Abel's faith remarkable? What did he demonstrate that his older brother, Cain, did not? And more importantly, what lesson(s) of faith can your pilgrim learn from our Lord's first martyr?

As you may recall, Abel kept flocks during his tenure on earth, while Cain worked the soil. In time, they both brought a portion of their abundance before the Lord as an offering. But as the prophet astutely records, Cain brought "some of the fruits of the soil," while Abel brought "fat portions from some of the firstborn of his flock." Cain brought a gift to God, but was it the best of what he had? Was it, as they say, the "cream of the crop"? Or did his offering simply fulfill his duty?

Abel, on the other hand, brought the choice cuts from the most precious portion of his flock. He gave to our Lord the BEST of what he had. And through the fragrant aroma of his offering, our Father looked with favor upon Abel.

Now your pilgrim's current state of doubt might be inclined to question God's "fairness" in this seemingly one-sided favor. For didn't Cain and Abel both bring an offering? Cain worked the soil; as a result, he may not have possessed a lamb for the slaughter. Was he destined to failure before he began? Does God care only for the smoke of rams and not the fruit of the land?

In His infallible foreknowledge, however, our Lord anticipated this petty line of reasoning. He directly addressed Cain's discontent over Heaven's unilateral pleasure. Our Lord said to Cain, "Why are you angry? If you do what is right, will you not be accepted? But if you do not do what is right, sin is crouching at your door; it desires to have you, but you must master it."

At this juncture, you must be sure to point out to your pilgrim that Cain had the opportunity to do what is right. Indeed, all men do. (Incidentally, isn't man's "fairness" complex peculiar, Barnabas? Even their snot-nosed toddlers spew that sniveling nonsense! Where do they learn it? For justice I can understand. Heaven's halls ring with our Lord's justice. He is just. But "fairness"? In Heaven we've never troubled ourselves with such a trifle. "Fair" is nothing but a wicked perversion of our enemy, meant to derail gratitude...but I digress.)

Our Father made it clear in Cain's case that the offering itself—grain or lamb—had nothing to do with His pleasure. Every man, no matter his occupation, social position, or possessions can come to the Lord. The difference in the brothers' offerings, however, visibly demonstrated a difference in their hearts.

Here lies one of the primary principles of faith: the heart of the matter lies in the heart. An offering is simply an offering. It can be given to God in loveless duty or from the gratitude of a loving heart. That motive force makes all the difference. The widow's penny may speak more loudly than the rich man's millions, because her heart is in her hand. Stress this point, dear Barnabas! For while men look at the outward appearance, our Lord looks at the heart. He knows when His children come near with their mouths, but their hearts remain far.

Perhaps you also recall the words of our cousin Samuel to the young King Saul? The prophet said, "Does the Lord delight in burnt offerings and sacrifices as much as in obeying the voice of the Lord? To obey is better than sacrifice, and to heed is better than the fat of rams." Here your pilgrim should see how obedience to the Spirit's voice must supersede sacrifice. Faith without works is not faith; but works may come without genuine faith.

But what if your pilgrim then objects: "Even if Cain didn't bring the best of what he had, didn't he obey by bringing an offering?" To which you must be ready to pivot your approach. Respond by differentiating between compulsion and a gift of love. For motive makes meaning!

25

God looks at the intentions of the heart. You must remind your pilgrim, Barnabas, of our Lord's words to His disciples on the topic of obedience.

True obedience is an act of love. The one who loves, unlike Cain, gives his lover the BEST of who is he and what he has. Otherwise, the affection is not true love; and the act is not obedience, but only loveless duty. The obedient servant is the man, who like David, recognizes an offering is meaningless without a broken spirit and contrite heart.

But did Cain's petulant anger at God demonstrate brokenness? Did the injured pride displayed on his downcast face belie a contrite heart? Hardly. So it's clear: Cain failed because his heart was not right; Abel succeeded because his faith was full of his heart.

Only the heart will find God, Barnabas. For a man's mind may find a great many reasons for serving our Lord. Some of these justifications may be pure, others selfish. But reason alone will never entice a man to crucify himself with Christ. Only the unfathomable reasoning of love will cause him to embrace the death that gives him life. Abel gave his heart to God; it cost him his life on earth. But in his sacrifice of faith, he became a true worshiper of God: he found the only true life.

Our Father has been repeating this message ever since He put His mark on Cain. Through

the mouth of His prophets, like Isaiah, our Lord has declared: "Stop bringing meaningless offerings! Your incense is detestable to me." And instead, through His prophet Joel: "Rend your hearts."

Of course, you also observed, dear Barnabas, how the Son was no less frank with those whitewashed tombs who strode through His Temple courts. Jesus saw the brood of vipers in their hearts; He denounced their hypocrisy and exposed the filth on the inside of their "clean cups." For Christ chooses not the self-righteous, but the man after His own heart—gentle and humble.

So what does this all have to do with your pilgrim's struggle with faith? To which I respond: Everything! For the foundation of the life of faith is the broken and contrite heart. And when the life of faith struggles, it is because the heart is not healthy, no matter how strong and vigorous it might pretend to be.

Remember the words of the Son: In our cousins' fallen world, it is not the healthy who need a doctor, but the sick. So your first task in reforming your pilgrim's awakening perspective must be to unveil the sickness of his heart. For unless he is reminded of his disease, and shown that it is beyond his own curing, he will not reach out for rescue, much less persist in the pursuit of faith.

This is, of course, the very truth our enemy will so desperately try to hide from your pilgrim. For the Liar will cause your man to look everywhere else for the reason behind his affliction. Satan will take all measures to prevent your pilgrim from looking within and admitting the sickness is his own.

But even if your man is able to admit he is not well, the Liar might induce him to seek a therapeutic alternative to Truth. For the pain of that incisive glance divides a man down to the joints and marrow. And he will do everything to avoid it. But when the Spirit's cleaving comes—and come it will!—you must be ready, Barnabas! Keep on the tip of your wings! You must be prepared to become the hands and feet that help lead your pilgrim back onto his homeward path.

With that word, I'll leave you to it! Make your first priority the condition of your pilgrim's heart. For only when you have ascertained the depth of its disease, will we best know how to nurture the seed of Truth the Spirit is cultivating in his weary soul. God will make the seedling grow, but you must be prepared to fertilize and prune its growth as He directs.

Affectionately yours,
Uriel

# Letter 4

Beloved Barnabas,

It appears my last communication has impressed upon you the vital importance of your pilgrim's condition of heart. As a result, I am pleased to observe how you have been working with the Spirit to diligently plumb those depths. For only a healthy heart will beat with Heaven's rhythm.

But even when a pilgrim's heart is in divine sync—perhaps especially then—living out a life of faith in the midst of a perverse culture can seem an impossible task. For how difficult it must be to be in the world, but not of the world! Perhaps for us, Barnabas, it might be a bit like being exiled from Heaven to the company of our demonic brothers. Can you imagine having to sit through those endless conclaves in Hell? All that vile jeering, jesting, and blaspheming—it sickens me just thinking about it. Their nasty antics really are oppressively tiresome!

Yet the pilgrim's divine calling is not too dissimilar. Indeed, the world he finds himself in increasingly resembles our enemy's camp. Don't you think? So understandably, a weary pilgrim like yours might be inclined to raise some of the following questions: How can a man of faith walk upstream against the cultural current for eighty or ninety years? How can he become a fortified city, an iron pillar or a bronze wall that stands against the relentless onslaught of the demonic forces? And even if, through some combination of grace and grit, the pilgrim manages to persist in faith, how can he be sure he has pleased the God he has sought so earnestly to serve?

When your pilgrim's heart asks these tough questions, you must direct its attention to the life of Enoch: the second hero of faith. For the quiet mystery of this saint's life helps to uncover some of the primary tenants of faith. And as you will also want to point out to your man, Enoch is commended as one who pleased God. Indeed, Enoch pleased our Father so much that he escaped death; by faith, he was taken up to Heaven. High praise indeed—a bit of angelic, fast-track treatment! The question then becomes: What about Enoch's faith pleased God?

Recollect if you will, Barnabas, how Enoch was the seventh descendant of Adam through the righteous line of Seth. He became the father of the fabled Methuselah, who is remembered as having lived the world's longest life. But most strikingly, Enoch is heralded as a man who "walked with God." Our Father's entire narrative only recounts three men who "walked" with Him. Enoch was the first of them.

But the ensuing question then looms large: What does it mean to "walk" with God? To which our cousin Amos responds: "Do two walk together unless they have agreed to do so?" So it appears, walking with God is an agreement—a relationship forged in faithful presence, intimate proximity and heartfelt fellowship. But most importantly, it's a divine union that only persists through grace and a one-way obedience: man unto God, and not the other way around.

Of course, you know our Father well enough, Barnabas, to understand that His Presence is always, in some way, "present." And so theoretically, any man might walk with God if he so chooses. Though it still astounds me, however, so few do! Perhaps this is because walking with God requires a life of unquestioned obedience. Sadly, how few men really want that! For what they choose to see is a series of concessions, rather than the love, joy and friendship obedience brings. But Enoch had the vision and courage to see through the demands of obedience to the loving God on the other side. In the midst of a perverse generation, he chose the companionship of God at all costs.

Yet before we get ahead of ourselves, we must note this point for your pilgrim: Walking together presupposes two basics tenants of faith. First, the pilgrim must believe that God exists. There must be an acknowledgement of Presence.

A man cannot walk with a God he does not believe exists in the first place. For as we have already established, walking together is an agreement of shared company.

Second, not only must the pilgrim believe God is who He says He is—the omnipresent, Great I AM!—but the pilgrim must also believe God is true to His promises. That is, that He will do what He says He will do: reward those who earnestly seek Him. For who willing walks with a charlatan? Who agrees to share his life with a known fraud? Without these two fundamental pillars of faith, no pilgrim will choose to walk with God.

But here we must also be careful not to underestimate just how difficult it is to claim these two prerequisites of faith. For while you and I, who stand in the visible Presence of our King, might struggle to understand how a man could not believe God exists, men have been given a great challenge. They must believe in the One they cannot see. Even those disciples, standing in the presence of the Son, struggled to believe in Him. Thomas had to put his fingers in Christ's wounds before he believed!

Yet every pilgrim since has been called to something more: To comprehend the brilliance of the Sun, when all he sees is the thin penumbra. That is not an easy task! But thanks to the Spirit's grace, some men like Enoch find in that sliver of light a glimmer of glorious hope—a reason for being.

Even when a man like Enoch has the courage to believe God exists, however, the call of faith asks still more: to believe God is a promise keeper. In other words, to believe He rewards those who persist in faith. This is much more than believing in that "watchmaker" God. To believe God is a promise keeper, the pilgrim must believe in a personal, loving God. He must believe God intends good, even when nothing the man sees seems "good."

On this point our enemy is a skillful and opportunistic opponent. He knows the multitude and magnitude of God's promises, just as he knows the weakness of men's faith. And the Liar will take every opportunity to exploit the differential. He will prey upon the pilgrim's doubt, impatience, weariness, entitlement thinking and selfishness to undermine any flimsy confidence the fledging believer holds in God's promises. The Prince of Darkness will attempt to portray our Lord as a stingy miser, rather than a generous and loving Father. Satan's minions will falsely present an indifferent and heartless God, rather than the compassionate and merciful Lord we know so well.

So on this battlefront, dear Barnabas, your counteroffensive is of utmost importance! You must be quick to intervene. Dress your pilgrim's soul in the armor of God to help him resist the devil's schemes. Help your man cut through the lies.

Only when the pilgrim is dressed in this holy armor, grounded in the confidence of God's existence, and readied by the hope of Heaven's promises, will he be prepared to walk with God on the arduous journey of faith. For to walk, as those awkward men do, means both parties must be in step with one another. Enoch was a man who agreed to God's cadence on God's terms. He got his life in step with the Spirit's stride. Here lies the challenge!

For many men may aspire to God's company, so long as it comes on their terms: present when He is wanted and absent when He is not. But though our Lord stooped down to become a man; though He put on sandals and invited all men to follow Him; He will not allow men to dictate the conditions of the journey. It is for the pilgrim to accept and obey.

Enoch chose to accept and obey God's terms. He walked with God. And his agreement to those terms wasn't for just a casual, afternoon stroll. He walked with God for 300 years! So when your pilgrim's weariness in faith struggles with its measly decades, direct his gaze to Enoch's centuries. Remind him that the same God who so faithfully walked with Enoch through those hundreds of years, longs to walk with your man as well. Our Lord's Presence promises: The weary will walk and not become faint.

That is...if your man agrees to the divine companionship. Because when a man chooses to walk with God, it invariably changes him. The longer he walks with God, the more the pilgrim will become like the God he walks with—for he who walks with the wise grows wise. As a result, your pilgrim must be ready and willing for transformation!

For some pilgrims, this change comes quickly; for others, like Enoch, it perfects over centuries. But short or long, oneness with Christ is the goal. Only when a man's faith brings him to this unification, will he be prepared to please God. In and of himself, no pilgrim—however hard he has strived and no matter how difficult his journey—will develop a faith capable of pleasing God. For to please God, a man must be clothed in the faith of Christ.

But lest your pilgrim despair—saying, "Who can take on the faith of Christ?"—you must impress upon your man the heavenly power he has been given. For faith is that divine dance between the grace freely bestowed and the costly steps of countless choices for righteousness. Without the everyday choices, God's gift is functionless. And without the gift, the choices are bootless. But through that combination of

Heaven's power and man's grit, the seeking life slowly takes on the faith of Christ.

Dressed in this faith alone, a man might hope to please God. In the raiment of Christ, God promises to reward those who earnestly seek Him. So in your pilgrim's hour of weariness and doubt, do not fail to remind him of Enoch's example. Bolster your charge's belief in God's existence. Encourage your man's trust in our Father's promises. And as always, point his eyes to Heaven's hope—the prize for which God has called him heavenward in Christ Jesus.

Affectionately yours,
*Uriel*

# Letter 5

Beloved Barnabas,

I note with pleasure the recent inroads your Spirit-led efforts have made into the darkness of your pilgrim's soul. For as you know, the Darkness has an insatiable appetite. It is gluttonous to the core—a black hole for souls! And unless the Spirit empowers your pilgrim to battle against those rulers, authorities and powers of that shadowed world, all will be lost. So be faithful to your calling, Barnabas. Help your pilgrim fight the good fight!

As you assist him in his battles against this Darkness, never forget the following truth: One of your pilgrim's primary enemies will be himself. That is, the darkness within him, rather than without. Or more specifically, the shadows that birth false fear. This form of fear goes hand in hand with doubt, and it has been a plague on the hearts of men since the Garden. Your pilgrim's current doubt wrestles with this fear. He wonders whether his efforts are in vain. But this pitiful feeling of "pointlessness" is a device of Satan; it is a corrupted fear that must be rooted out before it strangles your pilgrim's faith.

Recall the fateful events of Eden, Barnabas. How with his slippery tongue, our enemy induced Eve—and by extension Adam—to eat the forbidden fruit. At first, Heaven was on earth, and earth was Heaven. There was no fear and there was no doubt—until the first couple ate that fruit. Then, slithering like the snake, fear and shame entered the world. Adam and Eve hid from God because they were afraid. Why?

Didn't the first couple attempt to hide from God because their eyes were now opened? In the knowledge of good and evil, they became aware of their disobedience and felt their vulnerable nakedness before a Holy God. Sin had entered their hearts, and with it, as the prophet would later tell the people, the "curse" of disobedience: an anxious mind, eyes weary with longing, and a despairing heart—a fretful existence lived in constant suspense, filled with dread both night and day, never sure of life. What an awful state! Yet the world chooses to wallow in it like a happy hog in its pigsty. And to think—the first couple could have chosen life instead. What a tragedy!

Ever since the Garden, however, Satan has used this tainted fear to dominate the hearts and minds of God's children. For so long as the Liar can keep men preoccupied with the countless hobgoblins of everyday life, the pilgrim will find his journey impeded. His focus will shift from Heaven to earth, and from God to self. And instead of our Lord sitting on the throne of the pilgrim's life, suddenly the man's fears will have placed him in the precarious position of "king" over a life of trouble. No wonder he is anxious! For the bedeviled pilgrim might, at any moment, be toppled from his flimsy throne by a simple slingshot from Hell! And then what? When he has rejected his Rescue, who will rescue him?

Such is the tortured life of fear. Or, more specifically, what we might better call "false fear." For as you know well, my brother, true fear is an essential component of holiness. Heaven's halls are filled with holy fear! But this is a fear of a different kind. For as our cousin, Pascal, once said, false fear comes from doubt, while true fear emerges from faith. False fear is joined to despair; but true fear is linked to hope, for it emerges from faith, and faith is from God.

True fear is holy fear. It is what we angels exhibit every day: a reverent awe and respect, filled with love, and marked by obedience. It is the kind of fear that recognizes God as King, and chooses to bow before the will of Him who holds all other fears in the palm of His hand. The man who is filled with this holy fear has no place to fear anything else. He is overcome by the inviolable peace of Heaven. For when God is King, everything and everyone else is subject to His grace and protection or His condemnation and wrath.

With this truth in mind, let's return to that epistle to the Hebrews. For in your pilgrim's tutelage, the next hero of faith recounted in that letter is our courageous cousin Noah. Perhaps no saint's life better demonstrates for your pilgrim the power of holy fear to transform the life of faith than the righteous man, Noah.

Like his ancestor Enoch, Noah was a blameless man living in a wicked world. And like Enoch, he chose to walk with God in the midst of this perversity. Though the Lord was grieved with man's wickedness, Noah found favor in the eyes of our Lord because his heart was filled with holy fear. His life was a diamond in the rough.

But this jewel of faith only emerged through the forces of great challenge. For Noah was asked to believe the unbelievable, and to do the unfathomable: To build an ark to save the creatures of the world from an apocalyptic flood. He was asked to put his reverent fear of God above all other temporal fears; he was asked to place it above reason itself.

Now as you and I know, Barnabas, the rational faculties of most men would have laughed at this idea. For as we have witnessed many times, man's reasoning is woefully finite. It so often fails to grasp the deep purposes of God. And the Spirit's leadings may feel like fanciful nonsense. So the warning Noah received from

Heaven must have seemed preposterous on many levels.

For first of all, why would a loving God destroy the very creatures He so carefully created? Why would our compassionate Lord punish the violence of the earth with unimaginable violence? Is He a hypocrite like the men He created? And further, how could God expect a man like Noah to begin constructing (what must have seemed to him at the time) a ridiculously large and unnecessary ship for an arid land, drenched in sun? Did God want Noah to be accused of lunacy? Would it bring our Lord glory to have the world consider His servant a madman? Such were the questions that might have wandered into the mind of an ordinary man.

Yet, as the prophet reminds us, Noah was no ordinary man. In holy fear, he embraced the absurd. He took God at His word; and he did everything just as the Lord commanded. So here you must pause with your pilgrim to stress the nature of reverent fear—it chooses to believe the unbelievable, and obey the inexplicable. Holy fear is filled with a humility that recognizes the borders of its finite understanding. It is willing to cross those boundaries with the courage of obedience, even when (especially when!) the particular act of obedience—like building an ark for a coming world-wide flood—seems ridiculous.

Because of this remarkable obedience, however, Noah, his family, and the representative creatures of the world, were saved from the waters that destroyed the earth. Because of Noah's faithfulness, God remembered him. As the waters receded from the face of the planet, the Lord blessed Noah. Our King made a new covenant with His servant, and set the rainbow in the sky as a testament to Heaven's love and forbearance.

In the obedience of holy fear, Noah became a light in a dark world. He was filled with the Light that shines in the darkness, which the Darkness cannot overcome. Through his faith, Noah's light condemned the night. And as a result, Noah became the heir of the righteousness that comes from faith.

This is the second point your pilgrim must not miss in Noah's example: By the grace of faith, and faith alone, men become heirs of salvation. Noah was saved from the flood by God's grace, through faith—not as a work he achieved on his own, but as a gift from God, fulfilled through the work of obedience. Noah became the recipient of that gift because of his reverent fear. And through this fear, he was given access to the grace by which he still stands—as an adopted son of God.

But lest your pilgrim be inclined to think Noah is a singular example of this faith, dear

Barnabas, you must remind him: Christ has given access to this grace to all men, once and for all. Even a fumbling sinner like your pilgrim might reach through his doubt to claim his adoption rights. If only he overcomes in his belief!

So you will do well, my beloved Barnabas, to concentrate your efforts on this overcoming. Though the life of faith may be a constant struggle to believe the unbelievable, to the one who persists in his faith, God will reveal the gift of salvation. For despite the fact that the world will never see another apocalyptic flood, it will witness the final destruction of our Lord's wrath when He comes to earth again. And like Noah, only the man of faith will be remembered by his Savior.

With this future in mind, do not give up on your tired pilgrim. Help root his heart in holy fear. Fan the Spirit's flame in his soul so he might shine with Heaven's light. And as always, fix his eyes on the Kingdom. Like Noah, help him cling to the faith by which he is saved.

Affectionately yours,
*Uriel*

# Letter 6

Beloved Barnabas,

Your recent letter was cloaked in an admirable modesty. Commendable, of course, as humility must be a primary concern. But not at the expense of candor. For your words fail to convey how you fared in your recent skirmish with Trogglegot. He really is a foul little demon—full of cheap shots! He's always attacking our pilgrims in below the belt ways. No class in that nasty bugger! And in fending this miscreant off your pilgrim, I'm sure you had to absorb a few irritating blows. Such is our work.

But despite whatever you've recently suffered in this encounter, I'm pleased to hear in your pilgrim's recent prayers subtle notes of encouragement. It is obvious he is making every effort to hold on to faith. The Spirit's grace, operating through your recent war efforts, is unfolding its usual magic. Strong work, my brother! Persist in our Lord's power!

As it pertains to the specific approach of your work, I stressed in my last letter the remarkable faith of Noah. His was, and still is, a faith that empowered him to believe the unbelievable and to do the unfathomable—to trust in the word of God. But perhaps none of

our mortal cousins exemplified this power of faith more than Abraham. Indeed, as you may recall, Abram became Abraham—the father of nations and the Patriarch of the faithful—because of his faith. If your pilgrim is to persist in his journey, he must find inspiration in the life of Abraham.

Because Abraham's example of faith is so exemplary, however, we will do well to focus on one or two aspects at a time. No sense driving your man to despair this early in the game. For otherwise, he's bound to say, "I'm no Abraham!" and call it quits. Then you'll have double the work to do in reeling him back in.

With this stepwise approach, therefore, let's proceed to the first principle: Faith is a calling, and God is the caller. God called Abram, and not the other way around. No man ventures a life of faith without God's initial call. And no man persists in faith, without responding to the Lord's continued calling.

Unless a man understands this primary agency of faith, he may fall into one of two traps. That is, either a self-empowered—and as a result—God-less "godliness"; or, an impotent righteousness which reluctantly acknowledges God's agency and power, but doesn't lean into it heavily enough. And as a result, his faith fizzles out. Both of these types of "faith" fail because they do not recognize faith begins, persists, and

45

ends only with God. Our cousins are simply the incorrigible (nonetheless, irritatingly loveable!) muddles through which faith is worked out. So your pilgrim must never forget the fountainhead of his faith—from the moment of his calling, to the moment of ascension.

But I digress. For as I began saying, Abram's story demonstrates how this genuine faith begins with the calling. While Abram was in Haran, God spoke: "Leave your country, your people and your father's household and go to the land I will show you." Our Lord then followed this calling with a litany of promised blessings. And as the prophet records, Abram left as the Lord had instructed him to do.

Now as your sometimes peevish pilgrim will likely point out, few contemporary believers, if any, receive a call from God which is as direct and pregnant with blessings as was Abram's. But this truth notwithstanding, you will do well to remind your man that the "calling principle" remains unchanged; for God never changes.

The love that binds man to God, begins with God. This love initiates the call to man, in whatever manner the calls comes. And only with this call, will the journey of faith begin.

In your pilgrim's post-revelation days, however, God's call to man will likely lack the theatrical impact of Abram's. Our Lord will probably not speak from the burning bush as he

46

did with our cousin Moses; or beckon from the blinding brilliance of the Damascus road, as He did for the zealous Saul. And instead of a clear, spoken voice, the call may more often present as a soft, persistent sense the man cannot escape. Rather than a single, decisive event, it may be a series of steps in the direction of God's whisper. For though Elijah looked for God in the wind and fire, the Lord called to him in the gentleness of a whisper. But whether fast or slow, loud or soft, faith always beckons from the Father's throne. It calls out to the elect.

Faith is a gift of God, given to the chosen by the Giver Himself. As with everything our Father does, He gives faith to His children with intentionality. Nothing is random in Heaven's economy. God makes no bad investments. And just as any gift has a recipient in mind, so also the gift of faith.

Yet unless your pilgrim begin to get the idea a "gift" means man has no part to play in this equation of faith, Abram's story gives the crucial balance. For a gift—even the gift of faith—is incomplete so long as it remains simply a divine present. For even spiritual gifts must be received, "unwrapped" as it were, and then put to good use in order to bring the giver joy. And here is where Abram's example shines. As our mortal cousin James points out: "Was not our ancestor Abraham considered righteous for what he _did_...?"

When God called Abram, the budding Patriarch responded: he acted in faith upon the call of faith God implanted in his heart. When the Lord asked Abram to pack up his life and head to a place he did not know, into a future he could not imagine, Abram did not protest or question. He did not ignore the call or refuse his summons. Rather, he obeyed and went, just as the Lord commanded.

On this point, stress to your pilgrim the following: Although faith is a gift of God and its power emanates from His throne, the call of faith does not have a foregone conclusion. That is, man always has a choice. He is free to answer the call, or not. Like Abram, the pilgrim may embrace the "Go!" of God, or refuse it. The pilgrim may pick up his cross and follow his Lord, or choose instead to spit in Majesty's face. Incredibly, God's immeasurable love gives man this self-determining power! Truth be told, dear Barnabas (and I'm not telling you something our Lord doesn't already know), sometimes this lavish charity irritates me to no end!

But obviously, our Lord longs for every man and woman to answer His call of faith. His heart's desire is that all men might be saved. Yet, in His unfathomable love, He has granted men freedom—even the freedom to reject Him. In His omniscience, He knows how few will answer His call. His Spirit grieves to consider how many will use their freedom to turn their backs and walk away. But praise be to our Lord—some men, like Abram, choose their Glory instead! And these pilgrims, whom our Lord has predestined for eternity with Him, will walk with God until they reach His Promised Land.

So as you continue to guide and encourage your pilgrim's journey, Barnabas, make sure to direct his attention to the calling of God in his life. Cause him to reflect on the divine draw of his first summons. Help him meditate on the power that enticed his feet to begin Heaven's homeward pilgrimage. For in this reflection, your man will be sure to find a God who loves him, knows him, and calls him by his name.

Until I write again, focus on these facts of faith. Attune your pilgrim's ears to the calling of our Lord. And may the Father, who calls us by our names, strengthen your every effort!

Affectionately yours,
*Uriel*

# Letter 7

Beloved Barnabas,

I left off my last correspondence exhorting you to pay close attention to the calling of God in your pilgrim's life. From your report, it sounds like your man is responding to your efforts. And good thing! For if any man will push through the doubts of faith, he must hear the call of God. The strength of a man's will, will not be enough to conquer the Liar's flaming arrows. For this victory, the pilgrim must harness the will and power of our King. And even the stoutest warrior of faith will not draw on that will, until he listens for God's voice.

But even when a man hears God's call—and like Abram—responds in faith, staying true to this call requires him to survive the inevitable exile of faith that follows. For when a man like your pilgrim emulates Abram's example, he suddenly finds himself a stranger in a foreign land. He is a knight of faith set out on a seemingly endless pilgrimage. As a result, the life of a saint is often a lonely one. It must survive the inexorable alienation of faith.

As a case in point, you observed how Abram packed up and left Haran for the Promised Land. When he arrived, was he met with applause and a welcoming embrace? Hardly. Instead, he found himself separated from family, friends and fellow believers. God did not give him a comfortable, fortified city to call "home." Rather, he lived an impermanent existence—a wandering nomad who slept in tents, shepherded his flocks, and felt forced to pass his wife off as his sister to avoid personal harm at the hands of powerful kings. In short, he was an alien in a hostile country.

Obviously, the details of exile will differ in the life of your pilgrim, dear Barnabas. But the central theme remains unchanged. A man of faith is always a stranger in the world of men. He will inevitably feel caught between kingdoms: Still bound by the body, but freed by the Spirit; subject to the kings of the world, but a citizen of Heaven; in the world, but no longer of the world.

Recognizing this tension, make good use of Abram's example to impress upon your pilgrim the normalcy (and frankly, the necessity) of his current sense of estrangement in faith. For of course, our enemy will do the exact opposite. He will attempt to portray the exile of faith as a needless punishment, meted out from a cruel and tyrannical God.

But this could not be further from the truth. And as Abram's story testifies, your pilgrim's current feelings of alienation are not unique. Indeed, the estrangement his heart feels

51

is simply the sign his faith has set him apart for greater things. For when the seal of Heaven is placed on a man, this man will no longer conform to the world. The Spirit's tenancy claims occupancy and will allow for no competing "gods."

Still, your man's inquiring mind might wonder: Why does our Lord require this alienation? And if the righteous man must—by definition—be a stranger in a foreign country, how can a man like yours be encouraged by Abraham's example? What spiritual survival techniques can your pilgrim learn from the faithful Patriarch?

First, to the encouragement: The alienation of faith comes to those whom God has chosen and set apart as holy. It cannot be otherwise. For God is holy, and when God comes to dwell in a man, that man can no longer conform to the world. He must be holy as God is holy. Your pilgrim should be encouraged to know his feelings of alienation mean God has claimed him as His own. The Lord has moved into the temple of his soul and is making him holy. What greater joy can your man know?

But as you are aware, Barnabas, the dark world your pilgrim finds himself in is anything but holy. As a result, even though your pilgrim has been claimed by God, he will feel the separation from other men. Will he still struggle with the inner tensions of his natural man and moments of temptation? Of course! But, in the conduct of his body, the thoughts of his mind and the aspirations of his heart, he will stand apart from the crowd. And so he must! For Christ in him will leave no other option. He will be like a city on a hill, shining in the darkness of the world's night—righteously conspicuous!

So no matter what corner of the planet God sends him to, the righteous man will be a stranger in a foreign land until his pilgrimage brings him home to Heaven. For whether Abram was living among the Egyptians or the Canaanites, he was still an alien: a righteous man floating in a sea of ungodliness. Similarly, your pilgrim's sense of alienation will remain until his ascension. For God has chosen him before all time to be with us. And as a result, the Lord will make him holy—even if the cost is trudging through the mess of that blighted world.

Let your man be further encouraged to know that his alienation from this world means a growing oneness with God. The more estranged he feels from his current culture, the greater his growing affinity to our Holy Father's eternal Presence. This increasing unity ultimately works to fulfill your pilgrim's life purpose: to love the Lord and to glorify His Name.

Abraham's legendary unity with the Lord blossomed as a result of the Patriarch's trust and obedience—both of which were built on the foundation of God's faithfulness. This is a point I will return to at another time. But suffice it to say, Abraham's faith in God's promises encouraged our Lord's ongoing protection and blessing. As a result, Abraham became a powerful and wealthy man who thrived in the midst of his enemies.

But while the blessings of God supported and encouraged Abraham's daily existence, the greatest pearl Abram's faith experience offers your pilgrim is his big picture perspective. That is, Abraham always had his eyes on Heaven. And here is our next teachable point: The greatest key to surviving the alienation of faith is knowing where one is going. A journey without a destination is aimless. And an aimless journey is doomed to failure.

Abraham, however, shows your pilgrim how to persist in faith by keeping his eyes on the prize. For even while he was living in tents in foreign countries, Abram was always looking forward to the city with foundations, whose builder and architect is God. In the apt words of our cousin Paul, Abraham was forgetting what was behind and straining toward what is ahead as he pressed on in faith toward the prize for which God had called him heavenward in Christ Jesus.

This forward-looking perspective helped sustain all the great heroes of faith. From Abraham to Joseph, and from Moses to all the prophets, the warriors of faith lived their lives on earth longing for a better country—a heavenly one. They did not receive the things promised, but they saw them and welcomed them from a distance. They lived their lives with the pregnant expectation of faith that one day they would receive in full the promises God had made.

So as you continue your work this week, dear Barnabas, do not neglect these particular points we've just reviewed. Encourage your man's sense of alienation with a reminder of the Spirit's claim on his life. Exhort his efforts by recalling his future and glorious destination. And as always, impress upon your man's heart this truth: God is not ashamed to be called his God, for our Lord is preparing a city for him! Christ has a mansion with many rooms, and one of them is waiting for your pilgrim!

The grace of the Lord Jesus Christ be with your spirit, Barnabas.

Affectionately yours,
*Uriel*

# Letter 8

Beloved Barnabas,

I delight in the creative solutions you've recently applied to assuage your pilgrim's sense of alienation. Enlisting Ariel and Cassiel to join you in your recent encounters was a shrewd maneuver. Your collective presence appears to have greatly encouraged his heart. And rightly so! For even Abraham needed those moments when God visited him in collective angelic form to encourage and strengthen his weary faith. Likely, even the Patriarch would not have held on to the seemingly outlandish promises of God without those manifest visitations.

This point then brings us to another aspect of Abraham's faith journey to which I alluded in my last letter. Namely, Abraham's faith grew in and through God's faithfulness. The more God showed Himself faithful, the more faith Abraham had in God's promises. For ultimately, faith is a relationship. And all human relationships are built on trust. But human trust builds slowly; and the trust that binds a man to God grows one demonstration of love at a time.

The climax of Abraham's faith journey—the sacrifice of his promised son, Isaac, on Mt. Moriah—best attests to this building power of trust in faith. For what twisted faith would compel a man to sacrifice his only son?  Only a demon-possessed man like Manasseh would do such a thing, unless a righteous man's faith conquered death.  That is, unless his faith reasoned a good God could even raise the dead if necessary.  And how could Abraham endure the pain of Isaac's pointed questions about the upcoming sacrifice, unless Abraham's faith trusted God to provide the lamb?

But this is no ordinary faith.  This is the faith of the tried and true.  For the faith that marched up Moriah was built on the relationship of trust God earned in the heart of Abraham over decades.  And although this sounds ridiculous to us—God "earning" the trust of man—nonetheless, our Lord has allowed the hearts of men to demand these "proofs."  Our King answered the requests of Gideon's "fleece test," not once, but twice.  And He caused the shadow to march backward up the stairs to satisfy the incredulity of Hezekiah.  Amazing how often our Lord humors the frailty of men's faith, is it not?  His patience is truly remarkable!

In light of this, your pilgrim must be inclined to see how our Lord repeatedly deigns to bow down and wash His servants' feet so He might win their hearts.  For Christ knows love is not love which sits idly by.  No, true love moves.  It has hands and feet.  It walks into hearts and works the soil of the spirit until it breaks to receive the Kingdom's seed.

As a case in point, God's love demonstrated faithfulness to Abraham in countless concrete ways. But the birth of the promised son Isaac stands as perhaps the greatest example. For Isaac's birth was a long awaited miracle. What might have been seen as an average occurrence— a son born to a vigorous young man and woman—was turned, through a period of prolonged waiting, into an opportunity to showcase our Lord's faithfulness.

What I mean is this: God spoke His promise to Abraham—"a son coming from your own body will be your heir"—but withheld the promise fulfillment for decades. Not until Abraham and Sarah were old and barren—"good as dead" as the letter to the Hebrews says—did God decide it was time to fulfill His promise. And what happened in those intervening years? Our Lord refined Abraham's faith. Our Father built a relationship of trust.

Even when Abraham's faith grew weary with waiting, and he chose to bed Hagar in hopes of getting an heir, God remained faithful. Despite Abraham's impatience, our Lord met with Abraham and renewed His promise of a son through Sarah. Even when Abraham laughed at our Father's proposal, God remained earnest: "your wife Sarah will bear you a son, and you will call him Isaac." Our Lord later sent three of our brothers to meet Abraham near the trees of Mamre to once again reinforce His promise.

Because of these repeated demonstrations of God's faithfulness, Abraham's faith deepened. So at the promised time, God saw fit to bless Sarah with the birth of Isaac. Once again, God's faithfulness proved itself faithful to Abraham. The Patriarch's faith was now finally prepared for its ultimate test: Mt. Moriah's sacrifice.

In Abraham's example, therefore, your pilgrim must be encouraged to see an imperfect man whose faith was slowly strengthened and refined by a faithful God. Day by day, with each passing moment, the Lord slowly sculpted a saint from the muddy clay of Ur. For Abraham's faith wasn't capable of Moriah's altar until God purified it. Likewise, your pilgrim's faith must endure the long latency of God's refining work. And you, Barnabas, must encourage and support his waiting on God—for it's one of life's greatest challenges!

This said, there remains at least one more lesson for your pilgrim to draw out of Abraham's Moriah experience. But time is short at present, for my attention is being drawn to one of Zadkiel's concerns. It seems one of his guardians, our dear brother Onesimus, has run into a spot of trouble with his current charge. Onesimus' man is a charismatic preacher who has gone wildly off course, dabbling with the affections of the women in his congregation. You and I both know, Barnabas, what a potential disaster that will be if it goes unchecked. A real powder keg! I've got to help our brothers get that tomfoolery under wraps quickly before it blows up.

For this reason, I will need to revisit our final point in my next letter. Until then, focus your pilgrim's faith on God's faithfulness. In this manner, your pilgrim might be encouraged to see how carefully and lovingly his Father has shepherded his journey thus far.

And may our Good Shepherd continue to guard and guide your way, dear Barnabas.

Affectionately yours,
*Uriel*

# Letter 9

Beloved Barnabas,

Your detailed account of your pilgrim's labors for gratefulness comes as a welcome surprise. For gratitude in the midst of weariness is no simple feat! It requires a man to deny self-pity and search for the good, however small and sparse its instances may be in times of trouble. This hard work on his part makes it clear: your man, like Abraham before him, is attempting to hold on to faith by focusing on the history of God's faithfulness in his life. Bravo! We're headed in the right direction.

With this small victory in tow, let's return to my former discussion on the lessons of faith stitched into Abraham's life. For in my last letter, I alluded to the ultimate test of faith: Moriah's sacrifice. We discussed how God's repeated faithfulness to Abraham empowered the Patriarch to believe God would be faithful to His promise—even to the point of absurdity.

Now what do I mean by this? As you no doubt remember, my brother, long before the birth of Isaac, our Lord promised Abraham to make his descendants as numerous as the stars in the sky. To a childless man, this must have seemed absurd! How could Abraham hope to be the father of multitudes when he had not fathered one?

But when Ishmael came through Hagar, and Isaac was eventually born through the long barren Sarah, God's promise must have seemed much more possible. Then our Lord did the unimaginable: He replaced one absurdity with another. That is, now that God gave Abraham the fulfillment of His promise in the son Isaac, our Lord then asked Abraham to sacrifice his long awaited son.

At this juncture, we must do our best to sympathize with our mortal cousins and their woefully limited mental faculties. For no doubt, from a human perspective, nothing could seem more absurd to Abraham than sacrificing his only son. Wasn't this the boy meant to sire God's people? What could possibly appear more contrary to the promise fulfillment of God than driving a knife into the very son destined to build God's nation? And yet, that is precisely what our King demanded of His servant Abraham.

So the stage was now set for Abraham's greatest moment; and in it, the final lesson your pilgrim must not miss from the Patriarch's life of faith. Against all human reason, Abraham reasoned that God would remain faithful. Strengthened in this belief by the history of the Lord's faithfulness in his life to this point, Abraham saddled up his donkey. With his son

Isaac and his servants, Abraham headed to Mt. Moriah. Because Abraham feared the Lord, he obeyed immediately, even though it made no sense to do so from a human perspective.

As Isaac pointed out along the journey, however, Abraham did not even bring a lamb for the sacrifice. The Patriarch did not prepare, as our fretful cousins like to say, a "plan B." He prepared no contingencies. Instead, Abraham set out on his journey confident that God would provide the lamb for the sacrifice. In spite of a seemingly absurd command from God, Abraham chose to embrace the absurd potentiality of the Lord's faithfulness.

But here's what's even more amazing: As the letter to the Hebrews records, Abraham "reasoned" God could (and would!) raise the dead Isaac (if necessary) to fulfill the promise He had made to Abraham. Again, we must understand that from a human perspective there is nothing reasonable about resurrecting the dead. It is flat out unreasonable! It breaks every rule of natural law. Nonetheless, the Patriarch's "reasoning" superseded the confines of normal human reason to believe God could and would do the impossible—raise his son from the dead. Now this is faith for your pilgrim!

On this note, let us pause to consider your man's particular case. No doubt, it will do us well to move beyond sympathy to empathy as we try to understand his current struggles in faith. For unlike Abraham—who found himself living in an enchanted world where reverence for the divine was not only reasonable, but normative—your man is living in a godless world where belief in divinity is increasingly equated, not with wisdom, but quaint sentimentality or lack of intellectual rigor. In the contemporary mind, the proofs of prophecy have been replaced with the proofs of science. Divine revelation has ceded to empirical testing. And reason has ostensibly been crowned king instead of God. Could you ever have imagined such a tragic muddle, Barnabas?

So while Abraham's reasoning of faith was and still is extraordinary, the reasoning required of today's pilgrim is arguably more arduous. It requires the man to make the choice for faith amidst a throng of sneering empiricists and flagrant hedonists, rather than a crowd of religiously-minded witnesses. He must choose faith before a whole body of knowledge Abraham was quite ignorant of. These "facts" create a tremendous background noise that can make hearing God very difficult. Indeed, for many, this knowledge makes the leap of faith too great. Or at least, so they say. Perhaps it's nothing more than a flimsy excuse to hold on to what they don't want to give up—the throne of their lives. Personally, I think that's the core problem.

But interestingly, none of the proofs of science can totally eliminate the possibility (and though they will not readily admit it, the necessity!) of God's existence and omnipotence. For scientific exposition cannot answer the most fundamental questions of origin. As you know, Barnabas, only faith succeeds here. And the man whose reason throws out God for a bunch of "facts," must cling instead to a faith in chance.

But what is that? For as I previously intimated, if we play their numbers game, it takes more faith to believe in the benevolence of chance than it does to believe in the grace of God. What irony! These addled men will literally twist themselves into spiritual pretzels in their efforts to avoid embracing Truth.

Yet though our enemy has used science as one of his chief weapons to debunk the purported "myths" of the faith, we will do well to turn his weapon against him. For arguably, nothing points to God's presence and power better than the scientific details of the universe He has created. Whether it is the fundamental laws that hold the universe together, the singular marvel of planet earth in a sea of stars, or the beauty and complexity of the human body, the details point to a Creator. And as His servants, we will succeed best when we use these details to astound the human mind into obedience.

Let us employ the stars to produce the awe and wonder of faith. Let us speak through the mouths of babies to instill the speechlessness of majesty. For born of this wonder, a reasoning that supersedes mere reason will emerge to lead the pilgrim onward in the journey of faith.

Filled with this of awe of God, Abraham's faith persisted in the reasoning that triumphs over mere reason. As a result, God honored him. Our angelic brother met the Patriarch on Mt. Moriah and once again reiterated the Lord's blessing and promise. Because Abraham obeyed, his offspring would build a nation. The Lord provided a lamb to replace Isaac.

Use this example in the life of your pilgrim, dear Barnabas, to cheer his obedience. Help him see in the Patriarch an imperfect faith that persisted in the face of absurdity. When your man questions the purpose and meaning of his efforts, frame them in Abraham's precedent: a man who walked forward in faith even when it didn't make sense. In this way, your pilgrim might find the encouragement he needs to push past the dangers of his doubt.

Now may the grace and power of our Lord Jesus Christ be with your spirit.

Affectionately yours,
Uriel

# Letter 10

Beloved Barnabas,

Do I pick up in the tone of your last letter a bit of discouragement? I certainly hope not! For although the men we serve can be discouraging, there is no place for discouragement in our line of work. We have the privilege of participating in Heaven's missions. And these operations do not fail! For if God is in them, who can stand against them?

Even Abraham had a sense of this certainty in his faith, Barnabas. In my most recent communication, we saw how this sense emboldened his faith to remain faithful despite the long latency of God's promise fulfillment. Equally, how the Patriarch's faith persisted before the seeming absurdity of our Lord's demands. And although it's not pretty, nor without sweat and tears, I am pleased to hear from you how your pilgrim has taken these lessons to heart. He is at least recognizing the importance of persevering in faith, even if he's doing it clumsily.

One of the chief ingredients of a faith that persists, however, might best be exemplified in the life of Abraham's promised son, Isaac. His life was a life of grace, from start to finish. And a faith that persists, does so because of the operation and outworkings of grace. Nothing more, nothing less.

From the moment of Isaac's promised conception, to his rescue on Moriah and the subsequent richness of his adult years, his life enjoyed the immense blessings of God's grace. In this richness, Isaac remained faithful. His life might, therefore, teach your pilgrim how to please God in times of comfort and plenty (...and as an aside, this is arguably when it is hardest to remain faithful. For remember our poor cousin Solomon? How tragically he lost his way in the midst of God's blessings!).

Further, Isaac's faith demonstrates for your pilgrim how resting in God's grace can empower a belief in two seemingly contrary (but nonetheless linked) ideas: personal relevancy and humble submission. In other words, your man might be made to see how he is both a precious son of God, and simultaneously, an insignificant servant; how he is at once of infinite value to God and Heaven's purposes, and simultaneously, in comparison to God Himself, a relative zero—a humble instrument in the hands of the King.

Now these paradoxical truths may be a bit confusing to your man. So let's break them down by first looking at the idea of personal relevancy. As I've just mentioned, I do not intend to imply that the man Isaac, in and of himself, was anything special. No doubt our cousin's life continues to be precious to our Lord, even now. All of our Father's children enjoy this blessing as His offspring. Yet the truth remains, if God wanted to propagate His chosen seed through a cactus in the desert—rather than Isaac—He might have done that. So Isaac's faith on earth was not remarkable because of Isaac's inherent strengths, but rather because of what Isaac allowed God to do through him.

Here is what I intend: Although there was no immediate reason for Isaac to believe in the fulfillment of God's promise to Abraham, when Isaac reached the end of his life, he confidently blessed Jacob and Esau. Why? Because Isaac trusted God's pledge to his father Abraham. Isaac was convinced the blessing he would bestow on his twins would contain the power of God's promise. Isaac embraced his relevance in the unfolding of God's plan.

Even when Isaac learned he had been deceived by Jacob into bestowing the blessing of the older son on the younger, Isaac said, "indeed he [Jacob] will be blessed!" Isaac's faith believed God's power would work through him. Isaac was confident in the prophecy he uttered as a faithful servant of the Lord. And what was the source of this confidence? Was it not the God of his father Abraham and the Lord's long history of faithfulness to him?

What does this example hold for your pilgrim? First of all, your man should see in Isaac the individual's instrumental value in faith. Now again, this does not imply the man of faith is special. But rather, each man's faith has a crucial worth in the hands of our Lord and His work of promise fulfillment. When your pilgrim questions the utility of his own efforts, remind him of Isaac's confidence. When your man asks, "Have I labored in vain?" draw his heart's attention to the faith of the promised son who grasped his vital link in the unfolding of God's story. Isaac understood he was a vital piece of God's promise.

But surely, Isaac's faith might have failed to believe in God's promise. He could have easily looked at his current scenario and doubted. Or equally, so ensconced in the blessings of his life, he might have questioned the necessity of holding on to a fantasy. Why believe in a far-fetched dream? Why not simply live in the good of the here and now? Indeed, why might your pilgrim believe in the amazing promises of God for his own life?

Yet if Isaac was full of doubt, would he have gone on to bless his sons? If Isaac's words were meaningless gibberish, would Esau have been so distraught to learn his blessing had been stolen? And if Jacob had no fear of God's promises, would he have bothered to lie and cheat in an effort to obtain them? Of course not! For even our enemy knows the power of God's promises, and spends all his energies attempting to derail them.

Isaac, Rebekah, Jacob and Esau all understood the import of God's blessing through Isaac's hands of faith. What Isaac said mattered. What God would do through Isaac's blessing would be no mistake. Equally, your pilgrim must understand: He is a man with a mission minted by God. So even when your charge doesn't comprehend his circumstances, help him appreciate his life's relevancy to our Lord's sometimes inscrutable purposes.

Secondly, and perhaps more pertinent to your pilgrim's current place of doubt, Isaac's faith persisted even when his way contradicted God's predestined plan. For clearly, Isaac's preference fell on Esau. Isaac was a lover of the open country, and the mere smell of Esau's clothes delighted the aged father. Isaac would have preferred to give Esau the blessing of the first son.

But our Lord had different plans. He intended for Jacob to become the father of His budding nation, Israel. So through the deception of the younger son, Isaac bestowed his blessing on Jacob rather than Esau.

When Isaac learned he had been deceived, he did not renege on his blessing, however. Rather, in humble submission, he embraced the sovereignty of God's decision, even as he trembled before its power. Isaac recognized his role as an instrument of God's promise fulfillment; and in submission, he decided to bestow a fitting blessing on Esau as well.

Therefore, when your pilgrim's faith struggles with events that do not unfold according to his plans, draw his attention to Isaac. Help him behold a faith that humbly embraced the sovereignty of God and His often unconventional plans. Likewise, encourage your man to see himself as a vital instrument of faith in the hands of a loving God whose grace is always working for the greater good. Cause your charge, like Isaac, to rest in this grace. For when he does, he will find the strength to continue in faith. Finally, as your pilgrim persists in this faith, remind him: The testing of his faith produces perseverance; and perseverance must finish its work so that his faith will be mature and complete, not lacking anything.

With this exhortation I will leave you, my brother, trusting the Spirit to guide, guard, and empower your worthy work.

Affectionately yours,
Uriel

# Letter 11

Beloved Barnabas,

So you say despite your recent hard work, your pilgrim has had a temporary setback? The difficulties at work, coupled with his loneliness of heart, have caused him to again question the perseverance we recently discussed? Is that so....

Well, take heart, Barnabas! Do not allow this backsliding to discourage your efforts. For the homeward journey is never a linear one. Indeed, I question the man who claims a straight shot into the sky. His self-propelled rocket will soon run out of gas, and his mission plummet into the sea. For the war is not won without losing a few skirmishes. In today's defeat, find the lessons for tomorrow's victory.

To this end, redouble your efforts with a focus on the next hero of faith: Jacob. For if any of our cousins' lives ought to encourage the fumbling faith of your man, Jacob's life might well do it. He was, much like your pilgrim, a man of redeemed contrasts.

Think on Jacob's life: How he is the younger son who skillfully connives his way into the blessing of the older son. How he speaks with God at the foot of Heaven's staircase, only to audaciously bargain with Heaven the terms of his future faithfulness. How he wrestles with the Lord so persistently that he receives a blessing upon his disjointed life. And how even the deceiver of men is himself deceived by his own sons, as he is sold the lie of Joseph's bloody death.

Through all these events, our Lord creates a showpiece of brokenness. That is, in Jacob, God demonstrates how He redeems and sanctifies the natural man through a life of faith. The young Jacob—a conniving and willful rascal—becomes the wizened father of Israel's twelve tribes. The deceiver is transformed into the faithful believer.

Concentrate your efforts, therefore, on using the reclamation of Jacob's natural man to advantage in the life of your pilgrim. May he be encouraged to see in Jacob a young man who—not unlike your pilgrim—struggles with the plans of God, and yet holds on to receive the Lord's blessing. Not only does he receive God's blessing, however, but more importantly, he becomes one who blesses others. He is transformed, like his father Isaac, into a vessel of promise fulfillment.

We see this come to fruition when Jacob nears the end of his life. He blesses Joseph's sons, Ephraim and Manasseh, adopting them into his family. Not unlike his own experience, Jacob blesses the younger son over the older son. And although he could not even see the boys, by faith Israel trusts in the word of God. He places his benediction on the sons who would become essential components of the Lord's promise.

Perhaps the greatest lessons from Jacob's life, however, can be drawn from that other small detail the letter records. Namely, Jacob worships as he leans upon his staff. Several points for your pilgrim to appreciate here: First of all, the Word says Jacob "worshiped." The life of faith is a worshipful one. Like Jacob's, it is capable of looking back on years of disappointment, sorrow, famine and plenty alike, and finding in it all, the gracious love, provision, and sovereignty of God. Faith chooses gratitude over grumbling. It elects praise rather than bitterness. Make a point, Barnabas, of encouraging this worshipful spirit of faith in your pilgrim.

Second, your man should observe how Jacob leans on his staff. That is, he bows down. Even the Patriarch understands the importance of genuflecting before the majesty of God and His sovereignty. The life of faith recognizes the power of the bow, and will not fail to lean forward toward the throne of grace.

Finally, your man should not miss the staff Jacob leans upon. For the staff represents the journey—the pilgrimage of faith. And for Jacob, much like your man, it is a journey encumbered by the limp of faith. For when God touches Jacob's hip, He leaves Jacob with the limp of divine brokenness. No man follows after God until he is likewise "broken." His outer shell must be crushed. When a pilgrim is broken in this way, however, then the staff of God—with its supporting and shepherding effects—becomes the essential support needed to lead the limping Jacob (your pilgrim too!) through the remaining years of his life.

In these details, Barnabas, you will do well to help your pilgrim reflect upon the touch of God in his own life. Help him frame his personal limp of faith with Jacob's perspective. Encourage your charge to recognize the staff of God's guidance. Tell him that it is not only okay, but frankly necessary, for him to lean upon that staff as he looks forward to the final fulfillment of God's promise.

In this way, continue to minister to the soul of your precious charge. May the Spirit's grace and power move through your tireless efforts so that your man, like Jacob before him, may end his life worshiping the Lord as he leans upon the staff of faith.

Affectionately yours,
*Uriel*

# Letter 12

Beloved Barnabas,

Your comments on my previous correspondence are well received, my brother. Obviously, you've been acquiring a discerning spiritual palate of late, and I'm tickled pink to observe it! Speaking of which, as it relates to my letter, you'll recall we looked at the faith of Jacob—a man transformed from a conniving rascal into a worshipful and wizened patriarch. During this exploration, I made passing note to Jacob's recognition of God's sovereignty. More on that now. For a faith that does not rest in the sovereignty of God, will not survive.

Your pilgrim, dear Barnabas, must grasp how an enduring faith like Jacob's is rooted in a knowledge of the Lord's supremacy and loving jurisdiction over all things. The faith that persists sees the Father's hand in every detail. It trusts that no matter how difficult or inexplicable the challenges might be, God is working all things for the good.

This perspective is one of the most important, and yet most elusive, truths of faith. When a pilgrim like yours struggles with the doubts of faith, it invariably means he is wrestling with this notion of God's loving *sovereignty over the details of his life. But you must show him—God is in the details!*

*Even so, it is one thing to believe that God is in control of all things, big and small. But it is quite another to simultaneously believe that God's love wills to work all things for the good of those who call upon His name. For there is no getting away from the fact that human life is full of suffering—God's children notwithstanding. So in connecting the dots, a pilgrim must assume God uses even suffering for the good. That can be a hard pill to swallow, however, particularly in the midst of deep sorrow or gut-wrenching pain.*

*Yet to show the transformative power of this perspective, there is perhaps no better encouragement in faith than the life of Joseph— the next hero recounted in the Hebrews' hall of faith. For Joseph's earthly life was truly remarkable. He was a bright, handsome, talented and favored boy: the envy of his brothers and the apple of his father's eye. He was blessed to the point of cursing. But the boy who might have enjoyed easy success in life became the victim of man's jealousy and spite, even as he was the object of God's sovereign designs.*

*For who would have imagined a loving God would allow Joseph to be thrown into a dry cistern, estranged from his family, and sold off as a slave to wandering merchants? What man could see the hand of God in a seducing woman* and the years of an ensuing prison sentence? Greater still, how few could imagine holding on to faith when Joseph was honored by men and given unparalleled power over the greatest empire of the known world? And yet, through it all, Joseph's faith persisted. He was capable of recognizing the sovereign control of God in all the details of his life!

So when your pilgrim's faith questions his own place in life, dear Barnabas, point him to Joseph's faithfulness in the house of Potiphar. When your man doubts the goodness of God, remind him of Joseph's favor in the dungeon of Pharaoh. And when your charge is honored by the manipulative plaudits of men, draw his attention to the unwavering conviction of the Hebrew slave—elevated to prime statesman—who humbly used his power to fulfill the purposes God revealed to him.

Make it plain to your pilgrim: Through it all, Joseph understood God's sovereign control over the events of his life. Were there moments when Joseph doubted? Did he cry out to God in the cistern? Might he have been tempted by the sensual beauty of Potiphar's wife? Was he possibly discouraged in the dungeon? Or was he saddened by the absence of his family? Of course! Like your man, Joseph was a man—full of the desires of the flesh and the feebleness of human faith. But despite these weak moments, by the grace of God and the trained muscularity of his faith, he persisted. So must your man!

The crowning moment of Joseph's perseverance in faith, however, came near the end of his story—on the heels of his father's death. When the Patriarch passed, Joseph's brothers came before the Egyptian ruler to seek clemency for their wrongs against him. And where Joseph might have chosen bitterness, he elected for forgiveness. Where the prime minister could have enacted retribution, he opted for grace. Why?

Because Joseph understood the sovereign grace of God. His faith grasped just how wide and long and high and deep the love of God was for him and his brothers. Joseph was capable of looking back on his life and seeing in the vile intentions of his brothers, the sovereign designs of his Lord. Joseph's faith understood that even what his brothers intended for harm, God intended for the good of him and His people. The favorite son of Jacob realized that Jehovah works all things for the good of those who love Him and are called according to His purposes. This is the mark of a faith that perseveres!

As you continue to shepherd the faith of your pilgrim, Barnabas, make every effort to remind him of Joseph's perspective. For like Joseph, your pilgrim's life has had, and will continue to have, challenges, setbacks, and moments when the purposes of God seem inexplicable. I've heard your man's ranting and raving numerous times! All those useless punches he has thrown into the air have not been without a sympathetic audience. And then there have been those weaker moments, when we've witnessed his inconsolable tears. A bit heartbreaking (even if exasperating!) to watch, don't you think?

In these vulnerable moments, you must draw his attention back to Joseph's example. As the Spirit works through you, help your charge appreciate the loving sovereignty the Lord worked in and through Joseph's life. In this way, cause your pilgrim to reflect upon his own life and the Lord's control over its details, great and small. For in those details, your man will be sure to unveil a Father who loves him more than he could ever imagine. He will find a Lord who is worthy of all his praise, glory and honor.

Affectionately yours,
Uriel

# Letter 13

*Beloved Barnabas,*

*I fully acknowledge your well-meaning concerns about your pilgrim's persistent skepticism. But riding the waves of his inner dialogue will be sure to frustrate and confound you. Don't trust the surface. Instead, focus on the deep current beneath. That's where the real movement is happening.*

*As long as your man is still engaged, your ship will reach its port. The real trouble comes when these men disengage. When there is no inner conflict, then there is true reason to be concerned. For when a man gives up, the fickle gales have free rein to carry the heart away.*

*Speaking of fickle, however, you mentioned your pilgrim is questioning the power of Joseph's example. Yes, we've caught wind of that in his prayers. Just recently, in fact, he cried out: "Wasn't Joseph an extraordinary man? Who am I comparatively? Didn't God lavishly bless him with the best the world had to offer? What of my life? I have entire categories that are empty!" Funny, isn't it Barnabas, how easily these men gloss over the painful trials of others as they focus on their own. Blind as a bunch of punch-drunk bats! They truly are self-consumed ninnies.*

Anyway, with such a one-sided argument, your man seems to be suggesting Joseph might not have held on to faith if it weren't for his innate gifts and God's splendid richness towards him. Reminds me a bit of the cheeky devil protesting before God about the blessings of Job, does it not! What's your man's angle? Have you figured it out? Is he jealous? Deeply insecure? Spiritually lazy? Certainly he is ungrateful.

But there is no arguing: Joseph was not an average man, and he absolutely did not live an average life. God did amply equip Joseph with everything he needed to survive his personal trials and save the Lord's people. But despite this rich provision, it's not like Joseph's life was without great difficulty.

What's more, would Joseph's grasp of God's sovereignty have changed if he was just an unremarkable Hebrew shepherd? Would he have failed to display the same courage in exile and conviction in destitution if he was a poor fisherman or simple carpenter, and not a robed interpreter of dreams? Does faithfulness require human strengths or an angelic visitation?

As if in anticipation of such reasoning, the Spirit's letter to the Hebrews follows Joseph's example with reference to the parents of Moses. The letter moves from the gilded throne of Egypt, to the humble house of a Hebrew slave. The argument migrates from a man of unparalleled

83

*wisdom and power, to an average Levite couple living on the banks of the Nile River. The letter's logic travels—as our Lord often does—from majesty to meekness. Why?*

*For starters, the Spirit chooses this descent in direct answer to your pilgrim's kind of protest. Namely, the Lord wants to illustrate that the courage of faith emerges as much—arguably more—from the humble as from the mighty. To reinforce this truth, God chooses to begin the life of His great servant and friend, Moses, in a house of relative obscurity. Indeed, the narrative of Exodus makes only one passing mention to the names of Moses' parents.*

*What this humble couple does, however, changes history. In their physical vulnerability, they dare to disobey the commands of Pharaoh. Together with the plucky midwives, they defy the royal decree to murder their son. With unparalleled courage, they risk their lives for a higher cause. As we observed in Abraham, the faith of these unremarkable people empowers them to do a most remarkable thing—an absurd thing really: save Moses' life for God's future purposes.*

*But unlike Abraham, or even Joseph for that matter, this Levite couple does not receive direct communication from God. Our Lord did not send us into their presence with angelic visitations or vivid dreams. No doubt, the Patriarchs demonstrated great faith. But they* also received great promises and unmistakable signs. Not so for Moses' parents, however. This couple acts in faith simply because of the Spirit's subtle leadings. They look upon Moses and sense he is no ordinary boy; and they obey the Spirit's prodding to save the newborn.

Now that is the courage of true faith! It believes even when it does not see or fully understand. It obeys even in the face of potential consequences. As the letter says, genuine faith is being sure of what one hopes for and certain of what one does not see. Moses' parents demonstrate this certainty. Make sure your man does not miss their example.

While faith always requires a courageous choice, this courage will ultimately be in vain, however, if it is not coupled with ongoing conviction. For anyone might be capable of a single courageous act. But a courage that continues, requires the conviction of faith. That is the real teachable point for your pilgrim in the example provided by Moses' parents. Not only do they defy Pharaoh by saving Moses' life, but by the strength of their convictions (and the shepherding hand of the Spirit, of course!) they persist in that defiance. They recognize a higher power than Pharaoh. They fear the Lord more than the king of Egypt.

At the risk of death, Moses' mother nurses the child at her own breast. Even when the child becomes too old to be concealed any longer, she devises a plan for the child's survival. In the reed basket coated with pitch and tar, her conviction of faith places the hope of Israel afloat on the Nile. She trusts in God's providence.

When your pilgrim struggles to grasp the point of faithfulness in his own humble life, cause him to remember Moses' parents. They had no idea who Moses would become. They certainly could not have imagined how their baby boy would be raised by God in the courts of Egypt to lead His people out of captivity. But in the courage and conviction of faith, they obeyed the Spirit's leading. They feared God more than Pharaoh. And through the obedience of their faith, they participated with the Lord in preparing the way for God's great exodus.

In like manner, your pilgrim is also living a quiet life of faithfulness. But one act of obedience at a time, he is working with the Spirit to unfold Heaven's plans. Although your man cannot see the deliverance ahead, convince him, like Moses' parents, his efforts are not in vain. God is using him for Heaven's purposes.

On this note, I'll leave you to field your skeptic's questions. But as always, the Spirit is faithful and will assist your every effort!

Affectionately yours,
*Uriel*

# Letter 14

Beloved Barnabas,

What would it be like to be without wings, Barnabas? Have you ever imagined it? To be not only earthbound, but bound in time; to be a plodding pilgrim on that roughshod road of faith. Whenever I read your report on your stumbling man, I do my best to put myself in his shoes. And for all my critiquing, I'm sure a wingless life is not easy. I would be itching to fly home!

In light of this, I am all the more pleased to see that although his road has not been without its bumps, your pilgrim nonetheless continues to stumble along. In the end, that forward progress is all that matters. One foot at a time, he is making his way home.

The cloud of witnesses joins me in cheering his efforts, even as they hope he will learn from their examples. None of this crowd is more enthusiastic in his support than Moses. For some reason, the prophet has taken particular interest in your man's journey. Perhaps this is because Moses in some ways identifies with your pilgrim —his principled convictions, his duty-bound thinking, and his heart for God.

Because of this kinship of spirit, it may prove fruitful to take a deeper dive into the details of Moses' faith journey. For the lessons his life teach illustrate some of the most fundamental tenants of faith. Although Moses was a flawed individual during his tenure on earth, through faith he became a man the Lord knew face to face. Your pilgrim could not hope for a greater privilege. Should we not, therefore, see what Moses' life holds for your weary ward?

As you recall, when the infant Moses was placed in a reed basket upon the Nile River, our Father guided that basket into the presence of Pharaoh's daughter. Of course, the basket could have floated anywhere, into the presence of anyone. But, our Lord decided Moses should grow up as the grandson of a king. God ordained that the young Hebrew should receive the best education and opportunities available. Moses should be trained in the thinking, skills, and opportunities of the "enemy." For when one knows his enemy, and knows the Power living within him, then victory is inevitable. And the rescue of God's people from Egypt was the victory Moses was being groomed to carry out.

But before the faith of Moses would be prepared for this monumental exodus, much work had to be done. For not unlike your pilgrim, Moses possessed great natural strengths. Yet those strengths needed to be recommissioned, repurposed, and refined for Heaven's mission. This purifying process—whether in Moses or your man—means faith is always a work in progress. This entails a constant refinement as the Lord perfects a man's faith for His purposes. As it was for Moses, this process is often grueling and protracted.

The first step in the refinement of Moses' faith was a transformation of identity. The letter records that when Moses had grown up, he refused to be known as the son of Pharaoh's daughter. Instead, he chose to be identified with the Hebrew slaves he was raised to despise. Moses made a costly and courageous choice: He aligned his life with Heaven!

You and I, Barnabas, may not be able to fully grasp the magnitude of this decision. For we are cut of Heaven's cloth and live outside and above the confines of earth's power structures. But from a human perspective, Moses' choice was a radical, game-changing decision.

This decision required Moses to turn his back on everything he had ever known. The woman he had known as his mother, the family that had come to love and support him, and the community of which he was a part, suddenly became second place. The treasures of Egypt were traded for poverty. Power, respect and majesty ceded to persecution, infamy and penury. Moses' identity as the favored grandson of Pharaoh gave way to a fugitive of the state.

In this decision, Moses chose his identity in the Lord over his identity in the flesh. This courageous step of faith is the first lesson your charge should draw from Moses. For although your pilgrim may not have to give up the power of Egypt, to be a man of faith he must give up the throne of his heart. No man builds a life of faith until he has abdicated his soul. He must die to his old self to find his new self in God. As our mortal cousin Paul has so succinctly stated in his letter to the Galatian Church: "I have been crucified with Christ and I no longer live, but Christ lives in me. The life I live in the body, I live by faith...." Moses crucified his old life so that the new life he lived in the body might be lived by faith in God.

Your pilgrim's journey can take no other turn. The stakes will differ and the costs may not be commensurate. But he must make no mistake: The necessity to give up "Egypt" for the Kingdom of Heaven will always remain. Like Moses, your man will be given the choice to embrace the "shame" of identification with Christ over the treasures and comforts of the world. He will be given the option to trade an eternal torment for a temporal one.

But as you have no doubt noticed, Barnabas, even after his first commitment, your man will be given countless opportunities to persist or renege in faith; to join the witnesses who have gone before him, or return to the pleasures of Egypt. Satan will come for him again, at an opportune time. And only the man of faith will choose to keep walking the desert road. For what lies ahead? Only God knows and only faith follows. Moses' faith followed.

Once a man like Moses has given up his throne, however, then a second principle of faith ensues: living for the invisible. In his own journey, Moses walked away from the spectacular edifices of Egypt into the barren obscurity of the Sinai wilderness. He turned his back on what he could see, and headed toward what he could not understand. Even though Moses could not yet apprehend it, the invisible hand of God was leading him.

Likewise, exhort your man to walk by the eyes of faith. When he cannot see where he is going, remind him of Moses' perseverance. When your pilgrim struggles to make sense of his current situation, help him to consider Moses' forty years of shepherding in the wilderness. While Moses tended those flocks, God was preparing him to shepherd the Lord's people.

So also for your man, Barnabas. In all the details and circumstances he doesn't understand, God is orchestrating His divine plans. The Good Shepherd is leading him. In the fullness of time, your man will also fulfill the purposes God has planned for him.

While your pilgrim waits upon the Lord, however, let him do so with the fearless expectation of Moses. For even though Moses was a fugitive of Pharaoh, the prophet did not fear the anger of the king as much as the power of the Lord. As we have seen in the lives of Moses' predecessors, reverent fear is powerful. It gave Moses the fortitude that steadied his course and framed his wilderness experience. Although the young Moses fled the arm of Pharaoh, the wilderness-hardened prophet of God did not fear the courts of Egypt.

Finally, the letter highlights the discipline of Moses' faith. When the Lord instructed him in the specifics of the Passover, Moses and the Israelites did just what the Lord commanded. Of course, Moses could have ignored God's warning and failed to communicate the Lord's specific instructions to His people. But in faith, Moses took God at His word. The prophet initiated the discipline of the Passover ceremony. The people painted their doorframes with the blood of the lamb. In their obedience, they were saved from the hand of the Destroyer.

What can your pilgrim learn here? For as he is sure to point out, in Christ the Passover is no longer a required ceremony. But the example it sets in the discipline of faith, the obedience that empowers the act, and the blood of the lamb that sanctifies and perfects it, still remains. No man will join the cloud of witnesses without the disciplines of faith, sanctified by the Blood.

To escape the hands of the Destroyer, your pilgrim must persist in righteousness. He must read and recite God's word, practice the discipline of prayer, and daily cover his life in the blood of the Lamb. Only in this way will your pilgrim's journey of faith bring him safely into the Promised Land.

Sadly, Moses' sin kept him from crossing the Jordan into the Promised Land. But his faithfulness to God gave him strength to look upon that land, confident God's grace would bring him into the better country prepared for him. This conviction was rooted in his identity in the Lord, strengthened by his trust in the invisible hand of God, and perfected by the fearless discipline of his faith.

Help frame your pilgrim's faith within these parameters. No matter the position or stage of his life, may his journey, like Moses' before him, continue to hear God's voice and follow where He leads.

Now to Him who is able to do more than even we could dream or imagine, be all glory, majesty and dominion—forever!

Affectionately yours,
Uriel

# Letter 15

Beloved Barnabas,

It's painfully clear that even our precious son of encouragement needs encouragement. So it's worth mentioning here, Barnabas—our Father has noted your tireless efforts on behalf of your pilgrim. In fact, He recently expressed His deep pleasure with your work. Take heart! Continue in the strength and grace the Spirit provides. And don't falter now. For the battle over your man's soul rages on.

In support of this noble cause, my last communication focused on the faith of Moses as it evolved through the three stages of his storied life. One of the most spectacular demonstrations of faith which emerges from this evolution takes place in the nascent moments of the exodus from Egypt. As Moses rallies the Israelites for their escape, he leads them to the edge of the Red Sea. But when they arrive, they hear the footsteps of Pharaoh's pursuing army. The people are terrified. They cry out in anger against Moses. He might have despaired—"What now?" But instead, the prophet's faith prevails!

Our cousins have this peculiar saying—"Caught between a rock and a hard place"—which I think perfectly describes this moment on the seashore. The Israelites have the "rock" of Pharaoh's army rolling toward them through the desert. And before them, they see a "hard" place: the impenetrable expanse of the Red Sea. Will the Israelites be crushed? Is all lost? There appears to be no escape and little hope for deliverance—except for the miraculous door opened by faith.

Here is where your pilgrim can yet again learn from Moses and his fellow Israelites. For faith is the force that finds a way when there appears to be no way. Faith is the key to unlocking the door men have closed on God's power; and it is the tool our Lord uses to set in motion the glorification of His Name. Moses' faith opens that door and God's power responds.

Moses tells the people not to fear. They are to stand firm and watch the deliverance the Lord will bring. The Egyptians who are pursing them will be destroyed as the Lord fights for His people. The Israelites need only "be still."

Now at this point, your pilgrim, like the Israelites on the shore of the sea, is likely to say, "Be still? Easier said than done! Who can remain still when one is about to be destroyed?" And from a human perspective, this response makes some sense. For when a man feels scared and helpless, the last thing he wants to do is nothing— to be still.

But here you must remind your pilgrim: being "still" before God is anything but doing nothing. Rather, it means to stop anxious striving and to rest in the power of God. It means to actively set one's heart and soul to the effort of believing, trusting and obeying, rather than fruitless worrying, fretting and panicking. This is courageous, hard work, not lazy defeatism.

In the courage of this stillness, God begins to move. The east wind picks up and drives the water into towering walls. Dry ground appears on the floor of the sea. While our angelic brethren bring darkness upon the Egyptians, the Lord prepares a path for His people. Through faith, the unthinkable begins to unfold before the Israelites.

But unlike our angelic host, dear Barnabas, the faith of these men can falter even when it sees signs and wonders it cannot explain. A parting sea may not be enough! For human fear can cripple faith, and reason can ridicule it to the point of foolishness. And although a kernel of faith may help divide the sea, will it be enough to keep the walls from collapsing? How much more faith must have been necessary to walk through those walls, trusting God's hands to hold back the waves?

Faith that looks back to promises fulfilled and victories won finds reason to trust. It finds strength in precedent. This assurance might believe God can raise the walls of water and even hold them back. But faith that looks forward, through a terrifying passage to an invisible shore, must possess something more. It must also cling to hope. And hope, for our feeble-spirited cousins, can seem a fearful, tenuous, and dangerous thing. For what man has never had his hopes crushed in the weight of shattered dreams? What is to keep those walls of water from falling and crushing this spectacular dream? What if there isn't another shore? What if the Promised Land is just a fantasy?

Despite such thoughts, the Israelites dare to hope in the God of their fathers. Like Abraham, against all hope, in hope they believe. In faith, they choose to proceed through the sea on the dry ground God prepares, with a wall of water on their right and on their left. This is a faith for your pilgrim: one that pushes past fears and doubts as it clings to the hope of God's guidance and provision. One step at a time, it chooses to walk the narrow road of implausibility.

What results is deliverance. For true faith always brings this result. Deliverance may not come immediately; it will not appear without the labor pains of trial and tribulation; and it may not fully manifest till Christ returns. But come it will! That is the promise of faith!

Believing in this promise, the Israelites march through the sea. When they reach the other side, they look back over the disappearing road to watch the walls of water fall down upon their enemies. The hands of God withdraw from the sea, and it collapses on those who defy the Lord's people.

Through faith, the Israelites are rescued. By battling the inner demons of fear and doubt, the Israelites unleash the almighty power of God upon their enemies. In the same way, your pilgrim must dare to be still before God, even when stillness seems ridiculous. He must have the courage to rest in God when fear seems unavoidable. And he must push past his doubts, particularly when reason attempts to rein in the power of Heaven.

In this way, the fullness of faith will be unveiled in the life of your pilgrim. The pillar of fire may illuminate his night; the cloud may cover his back; and the waters may divide before him. Trust may embolden his next step. Hope may inspire his continued journey.

With these words, dear Barnabas, continue to guide and encourage your pilgrim. Guard what has been entrusted to your care. And may the grace of our Lord be ever with you.

Affectionately yours,
*Uriel*

# Letter 16

Beloved Barnabas,

Since my last letter, you've apparently noticed how your pilgrim's doubt has been wrestling with obedience. Exactly so! For at the same time, he has been filling our Father's ears with a combination of questions and complaints: "Why shouldn't I live with my girlfriend? Every other man lives with his. That's just where the world is now. We're not in Victorian England for Heaven's sake! What's the big deal?" (Whaa-whaa....Cry me a river! Can it really be that hard for men to keep their pants on?)

Or I'm sure you got a kick out of this one, Barnabas: "How is it my brother turns his back on you, God, and you've done nothing but bless him? And here I am, diligently walking it out through a swamp of difficulties! What am I doing? Why bother? Where is your justice?" (Oh my...you do have to feel sorry for the poor sap.)

Nonetheless, how tiresome this insolent whining sometimes becomes, doesn't it Barnabas! And yet our Father, in His infinite patience, absorbs these punches with a loving smile. I never fail to be amazed at His unending forbearance with our carping cousins.

But no matter how surly your man now acts, the obedience and duty he questions must be educated. For the longer his illusions persist, the more irretrievable his heart may become. A callous may form which will make your work increasingly difficult. As a result, speedy intervention is needed.

To this end, let us return to our discussion of that noble letter to the Hebrews. In that letter, the writer reminds us of one specific event—the fall of Jericho—which I think will be helpful in demonstrating some of the finer points of the obedience of faith. For metaphorically speaking, Jericho's defeat illustrates for your pilgrim how obedience helps empower the conquest of the natural man, which then paves the way for God's promise fulfillment. Here's how....

Before he joined the cloud of witnesses, Augustine spoke at length about two cities—the city of man and the city of God. Like Jericho, the world's first city, the city of man lives by the standards of man—surrounded by the walls of self-sufficiency: a rule unto itself. But the citizens of the city of God live by God's rules. They live by faith, through the dictates of obedience and the operation of grace. The people of Israel, perched on the edge of the Promised Land, can be seen as members of this latter city.

The Israelites' leader, Joshua, is met by our brother, Michael, and favored with the Lord's promise of victory over the city of men. Joshua is given—quite literally—his marching orders: March around Jericho once a day for six days. Then, on the seventh day, march around the city seven times to the sound of trumpets. When the trumpets sound their final blast, have the people shout. The walls of Jericho will come crumbling down. Then go straight in!

To a military leader like Joshua, a plan that simply entails marching around the city behind the priests and the ark might have seemed impractical. Indeed, militarily, it probably seemed downright foolish. Shouldn't he be laying preparations for a protracted siege? How about constructing ramps and ladders to scale the walls? Perhaps cutting off the water supply? But Joshua doesn't pester God with practicalities. He refuses to question God's plan. Instead, he tells the priests and his people, "Advance!" And in faith, they obey.

On the seventh day, the Israelites march around Jericho seven times. When the priests blow that final trumpet blast, the people obey God's directive: they shout! The impenetrable walls of Jericho fall before their eyes. God gives Israel an easy victory.

What, you ask, can your pilgrim learn of obedience from this victory over Jericho? First, Joshua and Israel root their obedience in the strength of God's promise. Like their forefather,

Abraham, the budding conquerors trust in the promise God gives: "See, I have delivered Jericho into your hands...." Even though the victory is far from won, they do not doubt. They do not run away in fear, as their fathers did before them. They put one foot in front of the next as they advance in the power of God's promise. They are confident God will deliver.

But secondly, their obedience also advances in the fear of faith. Joshua falls to his knees in reverence before the Lord and His messenger, our brother Michael. In obedience, Joshua, the priests and the people fall in line behind the Lord's Presence, the ark. In the reverent fear of Noah, they obey in faith the seemingly ridiculous commands of the Lord: March around the city, play music, and then shout!

Third, your pilgrim should not miss the diligent response of the Israelites' faith. God's command does not require one isolated act of faith. Many men might pull that off. Rather, the people have to get up seven days in a row and repeat the same seemingly pointless ritual of marching.

So much of your pilgrim's life is also filled with similar tasks. On many days, he may feel like he is just (as they say) "going through the motions." But these daily "devotions" are the evidence of a faith in action—a faith capable of bringing down the walls of a godless city. So do not fail to encourage these dutiful acts of faith in your man. They help pave the way for victory.

Fourth, your pilgrim must recognize that the obedience of faith will not be without pain and suffering. This pain may come in many forms, like it did for those marching Israelites: the pain of delayed promise fulfillment; the agony of trusting inexplicable commands; and the physically demanding work of marching itself. But all of these sufferings are but the labor pains of a coming birth—faith's victory over Jericho. In the same way, your pilgrim's journey of faith will require the pains of obedience. But be sure to frame these difficulties for your pilgrim as the necessary contractions of a glorious and fruitful labor.

Finally, the fall of Jericho must remind your pilgrim of the love and joy of obedience. For ultimately, the Israelites conquer that city with shouts of exclamation! It is joy in the Lord that brings the walls down.

The obedience of true faith is powered by love. That love brings the pilgrim to the joy of obeying: he obeys simply because he wants to. Not because he must; not because he desires something in return. But simply because it delights him to serve the Lord in the love of obedience. That is the true end of the obedience of faith. And it is this faith, empowered by grace, which paves the way for God to bring down the walls of the city of man to usher in the city of God.

So as you can see, Barnabas, the fall of Jericho has much to teach your whining pilgrim. Focus the obedience of his faith on the promises of God. Root his acts of obedience in the reverent fear and dutiful service of faith. And at all times, inspire in your man that love which generates the joy of obeying. When he finds himself filled with this spirit, then he will be prepared to watch God break the walls separating his natural man from his spiritual fulfillment. He will be readied to go straight in and claim the victory!

In the grace of Him who has shown your man how to obey, persist in your work. Be the hands and feet of our Glory, until by His grace, your pilgrim finds his way to the glorious city of our God.

Affectionately yours,
Uriel

# Letter 17

Beloved Barnabas,

Surely you've also noticed, my brother, how the doubts of faith inevitably struggle with a sense of "worthiness." At this stage of the game, there's no way you haven't picked up that theme in your own man's chatter. An insecure pilgrim like yours asks: "How could God forgive a sinner like me? I'm not good enough."

But of course, you and I both know, Barnabas, that is entirely the point! He's not good enough, and he never will be—unless he becomes hidden with Christ in God. Then, no matter what his past looks like, faith transforms his life into the image of our Lord.

Few lives demonstrate this principle as clearly as the life of Rahab the prostitute. Little wonder, therefore, the Spirit's letter to the Hebrews includes her as a heroic example of faith. For she begins her story as a flagrant sinner. And not only a sinner, but a peddler of sin itself—a woman who earns her bread by selling her body.

Now we could wander into that morass of revisionist history the world has become so fond of and explore the "why" behind Rahab's choice to become a prostitute. I am sure there is something we could teach your pilgrim in that tangent. But that would be missing the point for the narrative. For it was not the social forces which compelled Rahab to become a prostitute that drive her story, but the fact that in the providence of God she <u>was</u> a woman of the streets.

Indeed, God's Word makes sure to reiterate her trade, time and time again. Of course, this emphasis is not without purpose. For our Lord wants everyone to know where Rahab begins, so that they may marvel at the God who transforms her and takes her to the place where she ends.

But what components of this transformation make Rahab's faith remarkable? To begin with, we must take note of her predestination. Now admittedly, this word alone may send your pilgrim into a tizzy. And it's really a shame how much of a fuss men have made over the topic. They are unable to let God be God! Does not the Potter have the right to make out of the same lump of clay some pottery for noble purposes and some for common use? Men seem to be under the illusion that Heaven must obey their worldly definitions of inclusion and equity. Bosh! What impudence! Even the Son of God—who has a legitimate right to claim divine equality—never troubled Himself with such nonsense. Instead, He willingly made Himself nothing, assuming the role of a humble servant.

Be that as it may, there is no denying our Lord chooses His people. His Word repeats this truth over and over again. In His foreknowledge, the Lord knows who will respond to His call to be justified and glorified. And whether men like the idea or not, our King has predestined those who will reign with Him in glory.

As you know, Barnabas, Rahab was one of those predestined for this glory. That is, God knew before the creation of the world, the sinner Rahab would one day join Him in glory. The spies could have come to any house in Jericho, or even visited another prostitute. But they didn't; and they didn't for a reason—because God had firmly decided Rahab was the chosen vessel for His glory.

Encourage your pilgrim, Barnabas, with this reminder of God's inescapable sovereignty and special election. What God has decided, that will He do. Even an unlikely candidate like Rahab the prostitute, might be chosen by God to help usher His people into the Promised Land. So too for your man. For like Rahab before him, he is also an unlikely candidate. And yet, our Lord has anointed his head with oil, and chosen him in Christ Jesus to accomplish the good works God has prepared in advance for him to do.

As you oversee your man, reinforce this providential election. Imprint it deeply upon his heart. Watch carefully that he does not become complacent or pharisaical as a result of his chosen status. But neither let him forget the amazing grace which has fallen upon him, nor the love by which he is saved!

Which brings us to the next lessons emerging from Rahab's example: a confessing faith and a faith in action. First, a confessing faith. After courageously hiding the spies on her rooftop, Rahab confessed to them, "the Lord your God is God in Heaven above and on the earth below." Does this declaration from the sinful woman remind you of anything, Barnabas? Remember if you will, the words of our cousin Paul to the Romans, reminding them that salvation requires a confession with one's mouth that "Jesus is Lord," and a belief in one's heart that God raised Him from the dead.

Rahab beautifully demonstrated this two-fold principle: she believed in her heart that the living God could deliver her from impending death, and she confessed with her mouth that God was Lord of her life. This is the simple formula that transforms a sinner into a budding saint. This is the two-step dance that turns a pariah into a potential hero of faith. Make sure your man does not miss the gorgeous simplicity of this divine equation.

But as our cousin James makes sure to point out, a faith that simply confesses and does not act, is no faith at all. And here is where

Rahab's example of faith truly shines. Indeed, like Abraham before her, Rahab is considered righteous for what she <u>did</u>, not merely what she said. For after boldly declaring her allegiance to the Lord, her faith took action: she courageously hid the spies in defiance of the king's edict; she shrewdly devised a plan to save the lives of her family members; she facilitated the escape of the Lord's men; and she believed in the promise of the scarlet cord.

In the courage of faith, Rahab hid the spies under stalks of flax on her roof. The king of Jericho sent her a message demanding the lives of the Hebrews who entered her house. But in a defiance only faith could empower, she persisted in her ruse. She led the king's men to believe the spies had already left. So the guards set out in hot pursuit, away from the hiding Hebrews.

After this clever diversion, Rahab's faith caused her to boldly bargain for her life and the lives of her family members. Her faith inspired shrewd action. For as our Lord says, "be shrewd as snakes and as innocent as doves." Because Rahab feared God and His coming ruin on Jericho, she skillfully negotiated the lives of the spies for the lives of her family.

Your pilgrim would do well to incorporate this kind of tact into his own faith, Barnabas. For the world he finds himself in is filled with slippery, crafty men—wily as the devil they serve. Only a shrewd pilgrim, supported by grace, will survive the treacherous road lined by these conniving characters.

When her cleverness secured the deal, Rahab then facilitated the escape of the spies. At risk to her own life, she let down a rope from her window in the city wall and allowed the Hebrews to escape. Not only so, but she further advised them on how best to lay low until their pursuers had given up. In faith, Rahab protected and guided the Lord's men.

Finally, Rahab's faith induced her to hang the spies' scarlet cord from her window. This was a conspicuous risk. But the Hebrews promised to protect her house if the scarlet cord was hanging over it. So in faith, she obeyed.

Doesn't this "scarlet" business also sound a bit familiar? Isn't it reminiscent of the blood over the doorframes in Egypt which averted the Destroyer? Like the Israelites who believed in the blood, Rahab believed the scarlet promise. In faith, she entrusted her life to the Promise Keeper.

As we can see, Rahab boldly professed a faith in God and then put her faith into action. Consequently, she and her family were saved from destruction. When the walls of Jericho fell, only the people inside Rahab's house were protected. But because of her remarkable faith, God honored Rahab with something even greater: She became the wife of Salmon, and the mother of Boaz, that noble saint in our Lord's human lineage. She was elevated from a woman of ill repute to the mother of kings. She was transformed from a sinner into a saint.

When your pilgrim's faith wrestles with sinful feelings of unworthiness, help him recall the example of Rahab. Lead him to be encouraged by the reclamation of her sinful life. Remind him of the transforming power of a God who is able and willing to redeem and honor even a social pariah like Rahab. And finally, stir up in your man a desire to emulate Rahab's courageous confession and faithful action.

With these points in mind, dear Barnabas, help your man continue to work out that salvation which our Lord has worked into him. And to Him who is able to keep your man from falling and to present your pilgrim before His glorious Presence without fault and with great joy—to the only God our Savior be glory, majesty, power and authority, through Jesus Christ our Lord, before all ages, now and forever more!

Affectionately yours,
*Uriel*

# Letter 18

Beloved Barnabas,

Do I gather from your letter that our recent discussion of Rahab's life has brought some perspective to your pilgrim's sense of inadequacy and unworthiness? Amen! How brilliantly the prostitute's story continues to model God's transformative grace and power.

But there is another hero of faith whose spiritual journey might be equally helpful in bolstering your pilgrim's flagging faith. Namely, Gideon, that reluctant, and at first glance, cranky warrior from Manasseh. He is the slow learner whom God transformed into the faithful tip of Heaven's spear. In Gideon, your man may again learn the power of weakness in faith.

Yet what do I mean by power in weakness? Surely a man who is "weak" in faith will not be able to resist the attacks of our enemy. But here again, our Father unveils His truth in paradox. For recall if you will, dear Barnabas, the words of our Lord to Paul: "My grace is sufficient for you, and my power is made perfect in weakness."

Gideon's story demonstrates this principle for your pilgrim. For Gideon is an industrious farmer from Manasseh whom God stoops down to greet as a "mighty warrior." Before our angelic brother's arresting words, Gideon stands incredulous: "A mighty warrior? The Lord is with us? Isn't the Midianite army presiding over us? Are we not captives in our own land? Where is the God who brought us up out of Egypt?"

With such impertinence, Gideon candidly questions God's greeting. But our Lord does not directly answer this pointed inquisition. For Gideon has something to learn in the silence. Instead, God gives the reluctant warrior a command: "Go in the strength you have and save Israel out of Midian's hand." To which Gideon responds much as Moses did to his calling—with a fearful deprecation.

Gideon's central mistake in faith is one which most pilgrims make: He attempts to calculate with solely human coefficients. Your man has made this error on numerous occasions. And inevitably, it leads him to frustration and despair every time.

But God has designed faith such that the answers to His equations always require divine variables, heavenly constants, and the Presence of the Operator Himself. Apart from these three components, a man like your pilgrim will never arrive at the right answer. His equations will be flawed. Like Gideon, his faulty premise will ultimately fail him. He will find himself frustrated, disillusioned, and disconsolate.

But then God thunders in: "Go in the strength you have...[for] am I not sending you?"

When a man admits his weakness and dares to obey God despite it, then he is poised to see the strength of Heaven unleashed. For the power of Christ is made perfect in weakness. And though the particular equation may not make sense from a human perspective, as he obeys, the pilgrim finds the proof of Heaven's calculus.

When a man has too much natural virtue, he is likely to rely on that strength and not upon God. But when he is weak, when he feels insufficient for the task, then the warrior is ready to find in God the power he needs to drive Midian from the land of Israel. Then he is prepared to fight alongside the legions of Heaven.

Our Lord hammers this principle home when Gideon rallies his troops to attack Midian. Much like any man might, Gideon gathers as much strength as he has to advance against the enemy. But because our Father wants Gideon to demonstrate Heaven's power instead of man's might, the Lord forces Gideon into a position of potential vulnerability. Thousands of warriors leave, and Gideon is left with a mere three hundred troops against a sea of Midianites. Gideon might have feared. He might have retreated himself. But in faith, he pushes forward, encouraged by the vision God gives him.

Standing around the camp of his enemy, Gideon and his men sound their trumpets and smash their jars. In the clamor, God enters the battle. The Midianites turn their swords on each other; they begin to run in fear. And God's power overpowers the superior enemy army, giving the battlefield to Gideon and his troops.

Use this victory to your advantage, beloved Barnabas. Impress upon your pilgrim the strength in weakness and the power of dependence in the life of faith. As your man leans into God, when he is weak, then he is strong.

In addition to this essential principle, Gideon's example might also remind your pilgrim of one further truth. More specifically, God's remarkable clemency toward man. For isn't it ironic how men criticize God for His harshness on the one hand and His apparent indifference on the other? And yet, from a heavenly perspective, if anything, we both know our God might be overly indulgent, lenient, and actively engaged with the lives of our mortal cousins. Our Lord is always, as they say, "All in!" Gideon's life is a perfect example.

For if we consider Gideon's call to arms, we first see him questioning God. (Can you fathom it—Questioning the King? Who amongst our heavenly host would have the audacity to do such a thing!) Face to face with our angelic brother, the warrior even dares to ask for a sign to verify Heaven's words. (Incredible! As if God needs to prove anything!) But though God gives him a miracle, and speaks directly to Gideon's resistance, the doubting Israelite stills needs further reassurance.

Gideon later asks for another sign. And not one, but two. Gideon asks God to wet the fleece and keep the ground dry. When God humors this request, Gideon's doubt pushes still further. He asks for the reverse: wet the ground and keep the fleece dry.

What does our Lord do? Does he smite the warrior for his insolence? Does our King reprimand the weakness of his faith, as you I and might think appropriate. Not at all! Our Lord indulges the weakness of Gideon's faith and answers his request.

Though God has said, "Do not put the Lord your God to the test," nonetheless, He allows Gideon to do just this. In grace, our King humors the warrior's impudence so that the power of Heaven might manifest. Your pilgrim should be encouraged by this series of events, Barnabas. For he can find in Gideon's example a God whose love pursues the reluctant will and pushes past the barriers of doubt. As our Lord often does, He stoops down to make Gideon great, so the greatness of God might live in the memory of forever.

As you continue to corral your pilgrim's wandering heart and mind, beloved Barnabas, make good use of Gideon. For like Rahab, he is another unlikely hero of faith whom God transforms into His instrument of victory. When your man feels weak, show him the God who strengthens Gideon. When your pilgrim questions the leniency of the Lord, remind him of God's clemency before the grudging son of Joash. In this manner, even your man might be heartened to believe he too can become a warrior of faith.

Until this moment arrives, however, stay the course my brother. Persevere in your calling. And at all times, may the grace of our Lord Jesus continue to work through your loving and careful ministrations.

Affectionately yours,
*Uriel*

# Letter 19

Beloved Barnabas,

It appears that despite our recent efforts to instruct your pilgrim in Gideon's example, your man is still—as they say—"dragging his spiritual feet." Your report describes a true sluggishness. But don't grow weary in your work. For this intractable nature is normative. Sadly, a lackluster will in men is the rule, not the exception. And though it is tiresome to contend with, we must draw upon our Father's inexhaustible patience as we fulfill our duties to our cousins.

In addition to patience, however, you will do well to leverage repetition in your efforts to reform your pilgrim's perspective. For not uncommonly, the same idea, presented in a different way, will finally find traction in the muck of men's souls. Perhaps this success results from timing; perhaps subject matter or delivery. Maybe a mixture of all three. But whatever the case may be, I would suggest the following: Let us attempt to enthuse your pilgrim's humdrum faith by giving him another example of a man whose spiritual weakness was transformed by God into greatness—namely, Barak.

Of course, as you may remember, Barak's story is inseparable from Deborah's. And indeed, the ultimate success of his mission is even dependent upon the actions of another woman, Jael. So the son of Abinoam is not remembered as a hero of faith because of some independent and exemplary righteousness. Quite the contrary actually. His greatness is his weakness; his strength lies in his dependence; and the victory God achieves through him emerges through a kind of spiritual teamwork which trumps Barak's trepidation and obstinacy.

This is not to say, of course, that the fear and stubbornness of spirit Barak exhibits are to be commended. His weakness of faith should not be applauded, but acknowledged. And instead, use his example to point out to your pilgrim how God can, and will, work through the intractable natures of men's hearts to achieve His glorious ends. Even in the midst of his own obstinacy, your man might be encouraged to believe God can, and will, find a way to victory. For what our Lord has planned to do, that will He do!

If we examine Barak's story more closely, however, we notice first off that he is at best a co-protagonist. That is to say, his story begins and is ultimately dependent upon, Deborah, the prophetess. Unlike Gideon, the Lord does not appear to Barak. Our King does not speak directly to the warrior. Instead, God sends for Barak by way of His mouthpiece, Deborah. And it is the prophetess who transmits to Barak his marching orders: "Go!"

Perhaps the indirect manner of this message influences Barak's conditional response. He says to Deborah, "If you go with me, I will go; but if you don't go with me, I won't go." Maybe if one of our angelic host had stood before Barak to deliver the Lord's command, perhaps he might have unconditionally obeyed. But I doubt it. For if you remember, Barnabas, Gideon's responses were equally reluctant and conditional despite direct communication from our Lord. So it is more likely that Barak's response is a reflection of man's general weakness of faith. Our cousins are in constant want of reassurances and proofs. What miserable faith indeed!

In Barak's case, this weakness of faith even permits the general to ride on the honorary coattails of not one, but two women. This is no small detail. For remember, Barak's Israel was a very patriarchal society. Women were not routinely seen on the battlefield. So for a general to follow the lead of woman into war—even the spiritual leadership of a prophetess like Deborah —would have been a kind of public emasculation. Further, Deborah even promises that the honor of the coming victory will also go to a woman, not Barak. This humiliation notwithstanding, Barak won't budge without Deborah. Such is the initial weakness of his faith, that despite God's "Go!" Barak is only willing to go with the help of God's supporting actresses.

At first glance, this behavior might cause your pilgrim to question why Barak is included in our estimable cloud of witnesses. Isn't he a failure of faith? Well, to a degree, yes. As in all stories, however, this sequence of events is of God's doing. For the story is never solely about Barak, or Gideon or any other flawed pilgrim. But rather, the narrative points to the God who stands behind them, and the story our Father wants to tell through their imperfect lives.

Therefore, Barak is simply an actor whom God uses to demonstrate another important principle of faith: namely, the faith journey often requires teamwork. For although every man is viewed as an individual in faith before a holy God—responsible for his decisions and actions—each man is also part of a larger community of faith which works together toward God's ends. Rarely will our Lord work His purposes through solo missions of faith. But rather, shoulder to shoulder, the Lord operates through His people to build His Kingdom.

As a result, draw your pilgrim's attention to his own teammates in faith, dear Barnabas. Cause him to reflect on those brothers and sisters who are essential members of his spiritual community: the friends who listen to his heart's cries, the brothers who help challenge and mold his perspectives, and the sisters who cover his beleaguered life in prayer. For like Barak, your *pilgrim's weakness in faith is strengthened for victory by all those believers God has planted him near—never mind the cloud of witnesses working from afar. This is a source of praise!*

*Strengthened in faith by his own spiritual teammates, Barak's weakness is ultimately ready to engage his God-given strengths. He races down Mount Tabor at the head of his 10,000 men and routs the army of Canaanites. Not one enemy soldier is spared, save Sisera, who flees toward the tent of Jael to meet his inglorious end: death at the hands of a woman who boldly drives a tent peg through his skull. As Deborah foretold—the honor of the day goes not to the general, but to Jael, and the Lord who delivers the enemy into her lap.*

*As you can see, dear Barnabas, Barak's story is yet another example of how our Lord takes weakness and transforms it into greatness. Yes, Barak's faith initially fails the test. He looks for reassurance where God has already spoken. But what man has not done the same? Abraham, Moses, Gideon and others have all demonstrated similar moments of weakness—your pilgrim too.*

*On the other hand, the general is not filled with a self-impressed and unreachable bravado. Rather, his spirit's dependency proves the fertile soil for God's pedagogy. For as our beloved cousin, S.K., has said so well, only the one who is* utterly dependent on God is truly independent. That man might become a true warrior of faith!

Make it a priority, therefore, to impress this lesson upon the heart of your pilgrim. Encourage him to see his dependence on the Father as his greatest strength. Like Barak, help your man value the teammates of faith God has placed into his life, recognizing they are essential components of the Lord's battle plan.

Finally, do not neglect to point out how Barak ultimately did his duty: with a faith equipped by God, he defeated the Lord's enemies. For your pilgrim will not be an exception. When his own weaknesses are empowered by God, he too must march forward to do the Lord's work. Duty will call. The man of faith answers!

With these thoughts in mind, beloved Barnabas, persist in your pursuit of your pilgrim's itinerate heart. For if we do not persist, how can we ever expect our sickly cousins to do so? Through the Spirit's ministrations, we must fill up that which is wanting in them, so that they may in turn fill up in their flesh what is still lacking in regards to Christ's afflictions. All this, so that the body, which is the Church, might be readied for the coming Bridegroom!

Affectionately yours,
*Uriel*

# Letter 20

Beloved Barnabas,

I can't tell from your letter—how did your pilgrim respond to our discussion of spiritual teamwork? In his increasingly individualistic society, a team approach to anything, much less spiritual matters, might be a hard pill to swallow. For their world is a cesspool of pushing, pulling, screaming and scheming. And teamwork amongst such a crowd of selfish children must be a true headache! So to make the medicine go down a bit more easily, it might be helpful to round out this group perspective.

Therefore, note the following: Although the life of faith will almost always require men to work shoulder to shoulder, sometimes our Lord utilizes His disciples in a more isolated fashion. In these instances, God may take an average man or woman, make her exceptional by the Spirit's power, and then use her to accomplish His purposes. We think of Mary charged with birthing our Lord; and Jesus' cousin, John, given the task of heralding our Lord's earthly ministry from the Judean wilderness, to name a couple.

But there is perhaps no more colorful example of this principle than the longhaired, larger than life, Samson. Whereas Barak teamed up with Deborah and Jael as he led an army of ten thousand men against the Canaanites, Samson was an army of one. Throughout his life, Samson battled the Philistines. But for the twenty years he led Israel, he never called his countrymen to fight alongside him. He led a largely solitary life. At times, he even lived alone like a beast in a cave.

A skeptical pilgrim like yours, dear Barnabas, might find reason to question this autonomy and isolation. Perhaps Samson was a bit of a madman. Perhaps his unbridled fury was simply an indication of his arrogance and self-infatuation. For if we critically examine Samson's battles against the Philistines, it becomes clear: Whether he killed the men of Ashkelon for cunningly answering his riddle, or set the foxes and their torches loose in the fields, Samson's vengeance was often personally motivated. Or was it?

Here we are presented with yet another reminder of God's sovereignty over man's choices. In the lives of Abram, Moses, Isaac, Jacob, Joseph and others, we have seen how our Lord employs choice in the development of faith. Because our Father allows men to choose, He works through their choices to hone their spirits.

This human freedom, however, sometimes means our Lord Himself is confronted with a difficult choice: Either allow men their bad choices, or intervene and prevent those choices.

But if God were to intervene at every turn, would it truly be freedom? Of course not! And men must have freedom of choice if they are to choose to love and serve our Lord. For love is always a choice, or it is not love, but compulsion. So it remains for the Lord to allow men to make heartbreaking choices; and then, in the depth of His love and compassion for His children, to redeem those choices for Heaven's purposes.

Samson's life vividly demonstrates this principle. From the moment our Lord visits Samson's mother, Manoah, we know Samson is God's chosen instrument to lead Israel and carry out His divine judgement against the Philistines. But Samson is a flawed hero with a problem: a passion problem. When he goes down to Timnah, he becomes infatuated with a woman there; he is determined to have her as his wife. Of course, this union with a pagan woman would break God's command. Rightly so, Samson's parents protest. How could they possibly imagine that God might be working His purposes through Samson's ill-fated desire?

But what do I mean by this? For surely God could not condone Samson's lust and his willful insistence to transgress God's marriage laws. Certainly, our Lord never blesses disobedience. But in this case, our sovereign King allows Samson's desire to proceed towards fulfillment because of a far-reaching purpose: Heaven's impending confrontation with the Philistines. As we saw in the life of Jacob, sometimes the Lord permits the natural inclinations of man to unfold in the exercise of his moral freedom, so that in the redemption of these choices (and their consequences), God might be glorified in the denouement. This calls for divine understanding!

Nonetheless, through Samson's lustful, willful, and impetus behavior, God finds the instrument for His judgement against the Philistines. Our Holy Father strengthens Samson with superhuman power, so that our cousin is able to slay one thousand enemies with a donkey's jawbone! (With such a feat, Samson seems fit for Heaven's army. Don't you agree? If he hasn't already considered it, I'm sure Michael could find some spot for Samson in the Legion's ranks!) But as Samson stands covered in blood and exhausted, he has enough self-awareness to recognize the Lord's divine intervention. The judge says to God, "You have given your servant this great victory."

As these incredible events demonstrate, our Lord sometimes works through individuals to accomplish Heaven's purposes. But Samson's vigilante-like behavior is no longer fit for your pilgrim's more "civilized" times. A man who brained a thousand men with a donkey's jawbone would be medicated and institutionalized in today's world! So perhaps the better way for your pilgrim to view Samson is not as a mythic spiritual hero fit for the movie screen, but as a kind of redeemed anti-hero. Now what can I possibly mean by that?

Samson's life vividly exhibits the constant tension in men between flesh and spirit. As we have seen, his life is set apart and dedicated to God from the moment of his promised conception. Nonetheless, he is still a man, filled with all the cravings of the flesh—a man of intense passion. Sadly, he succumbs to those cravings, time and time again. Though he is the strongest of men, he is weak. At times he is foolish in his spiritual resolve. Can your pilgrim not identify with this tension?

When Samson persists in chasing pagan women, he becomes willingly duped by the alluring Delilah. In keeping with our enemy's tactical repertoire, Delilah's persistence weakens Samson's spiritual resolve. For it is one thing to say "No!" once. But repeated "Noes" become harder and harder. Knowing this, our enemy plays this card all the time. As a case in point, Delilah's successive entreaties ultimately cause Samson to divulge the secret of his strength. She then betrays him to the Philistines. When Delilah fatefully cuts Samson's hair, the Lord leaves him.

Here your pilgrim should also take note that God's patience with man's disobedience has a limit. Even His chosen hero, Samson, is not permitted endless excess. God allows Samson to exercise his freedom of will. But in the exercise of that freedom, Samson is then exposed to reap the consequences of his poor choices. His eyes are gouged out and he is bound up and taken to the temple of Dagon to perform like a circus animal.

God does not abandon His servants forever, however. And once chastened, Samson seeks the Lord in prayer. God hears the judge's plea and responds. For the glory of His Almighty Name, our Lord then chooses to invest His servant with strength once more. Pushing against the pillars of our enemy's temple, Samson brings the roof down on more than three thousand of his enemies. Samson is vindicated and God is glorified.

From the ruble of this martyrdom, our Lord's name emerges victorious over His enemies. Although Samson dies as a blinded, imperfect and conflicted hero (anti-hero?) of faith, his spiritual legacy demonstrates God's ability to empower men to superhuman feats. But more than this, dear Barnabas, let Samson's example instruct your pilgrim in the importance of curbing the passions of the flesh. Samson is given passion for Heaven's purposes; and God uses Samson's passion to avenge His enemies. But that same unbridled passion is also Samson's undoing. Let your pilgrim be advised: The strength of a man may always be his greatest weakness.

Like Samson, your pilgrim has also been endowed with strength, albeit of a different kind. That strength is only strength, however, when it stays within the bounds of Heaven's will. For when it strays, a man's strength may easily become an instrument of the devil instead. The spirit is willing, but the body is weak. Although our King may choose to redeem a man's poor choices, those choices will inevitably carry weighty consequences. And like a loving father, our Lord may allow those consequences to transmute into the instruments of His divine instruction. May your pilgrim take heed!

With this loving admonition, I commend your man to your ongoing "TLC", dear Barnabas. May the God of peace, who through the blood of the eternal covenant brought back from the dead our Lord Jesus, that Great Shepherd of the sheep, continue to equip you with everything good for doing His will; and may He work in us what is pleasing to Him, through Jesus Christ, to whom be glory for ever and ever!

Affectionately yours,
Uriel

# Letter 21

*Beloved Barnabas,*

*I will admit, I'm a bit perplexed by your recent response. Do you mean to suggest Samson's example was a hard sell? Too storybook for your closet empiricist? The judge's superhuman feats are remarkable, no doubt.*

*Yet no matter how incredible Samson's tale might be, it has an undeniable visceral power. Even a man like yours knows that tension. And however hard you feel the effort has been, your recent tutelage has obviously given your pilgrim a renewed appreciation of the unrelenting battle between flesh and spirit. In this fresh awareness, he appears more motivated to dedicate his strengths to God before they career off course.*

*Obviously, the Father could not be more pleased with this rededication of heart. So I trust that through your continued assistance and the constant guidance of the Spirit, your pilgrim will continue on the straight and narrow. May he achieve Samson's victories without sharing in his repetitive follies.*

*But of course, as Samson's life demonstrates so well, the journey of faith—in the spiritual "goody two shoes" and desperadoes alike—is punctuated with folly. No man escapes. And it* remains for God's grace to make something beautiful out of man's mess.

Fortunately, our Father's glory delights in this divine transformation. His entire love story for man is replete with this message of reclamation. Never miss the opportunity to remind your weary pilgrim of these heartening thoughts.

Few characters in our Lord's narrative blend the heroic and the foolish as memorably as the adventurer of faith, Jephthah. His story is bookended in tragedy: On one end, he is the illegitimate son of Gilead through a prostitute—shunned by his half-brothers and driven from his ancestral home into the barrens of Tob. On the other end, his story concludes with the horrific sacrifice of his only daughter as the result of an impetuous pledge to the Lord. And to top it all off, he endures a short civil war with his disgruntled brothers, the Ephraimites.

But in between these tragic ends, our Father writes a story of faith in Jephthah's life which is full of a divinely inspired heroism. For like Gideon, Jephthah is a mighty warrior whom God commandeers to fight for His people. Jephthah's natural strengths are harnessed for the Lord's purposes when the warrior is extracted from his band of mercenaries and given a heavenly mission: Come lead us against our enemy the Ammonites.

Now the first lesson of faith your pilgrim might draw from Jephthah's life lies in his response to this shameless request by the elders of Gilead. For remember: Jephthah had previously been ostracized by these men for his illegitimacy. And you know the petty hearts of men well enough, dear Barnabas, to imagine how Jephthah must have felt; how he easily harbored a grudge against these elders. "Why would I help you when you've thrown me out? Didn't you hate me and drive me from my father's house? Why do you come to me now, when you're in trouble?" With such retorts he responds to the men of Gilead.

Nonetheless, Jephthah is not mastered by his bitterness. He does not allow his past to derail his providential future. In the grace of the Spirit, the warrior swallows his anger, resentment, and injured pride. He goes with the men of Gilead and becomes the leader and judge of his people.

Like Jephthah, your man has reasons to be bitter (but in truth, most men might claim the same...). Your pilgrim's past and present contain painful realities. As a result, he might cling to self-pity and wallow in resentment. He could focus on revenge rather than clemency, and retribution rather than lenience.

But the way of faith moves on in grace. It does not forget, but forgives. It does not pretend to be fatally wounded, but dares to turn its

133

wounds into a source of healing power. The man of faith, like Jephthah, becomes a wounded healer through whom God's Spirit works mighty acts of grace. You will do well, dear Barnabas, to focus your pilgrim on these truths. Cause him to reflect on his own painful history. Then, by the Spirit's guidance, help him see how God is redeeming his wounds for the advance of Heaven's glorious agendas.

The second pearl of wisdom your pilgrim might glean from Jephthah's example concerns the warrior's balanced leadership approach. He is a warrior, but he is also a statesman. He is able to wield the sword, but he is equally able to wield his words in the wisdom of diplomacy. As he should, Jephthah begins with the latter. He attempts to reason with the Ammonites as he recounts the historical truths of Israel's claim to the Promised Land. For as Jephthah knows, there is a future for the man of peace. Likewise, your pilgrim will do well to pursue peace whenever possible. Blessed are the peacemakers.

However, when the best efforts for peace fail, or "peace" means compromising God's commands, then there is also a place for war. For our Lord did not come to earth to bring a paltry peace, but a sword. And the true peace that passes understanding requires Heaven's blade to pave the way into the heart of a man. So when Jephthah's efforts for peace fail to move the obstinacy of Ammon, the Spirit of the Lord comes upon Gilead's leader. The warrior advances against the Ammonites and the Lord gives them into Jephthah's hand.

All this, of course, is not without the stain of that fateful incident for which Jephthah will forever be remembered: His impetuous and foolish vow before the Lord. Here the hero of faith is betrayed by the weakness of his humanity. His past still plagues him with a lingering insecurity and doubt. And instead of simply advancing against the Ammonites in the strength of God, Jephthah feels compelled to barter with the Lord for an assurance of victory. The warrior vows to sacrifice to God whatever comes out the door to greet him when he returns victoriously. But how could Jephthah not have imagined his daughter might be this greeter?

Yet you know, Barnabas, where this story leads: After Gilead's leader faithfully advances against the Ammonites and destroys them, he returns home to the reality of his foolishness. For who should run from his door to greet him? A dog? A slave? Was is not his only daughter?

Now the battle-hardened warrior painfully understands why our Lord says, "Do not swear at all," but rather, "simply let your 'Yes' be 'Yes' and your 'No', 'No,'; [for] anything beyond this comes from the evil one." In his weakness, Jephthah makes a vow; and as a result, he is then faced with a choice: Fulfill the vow in obedience or disregard it as an act of foolishness that a loving God must surely dismiss.

But Jephthah and his daughter know the Lord's law: "If you make a vow to the Lord your God, do not be slow to pay it, for the Lord your God will certainly demand it of you and you will be guilty of sin." So in the pain of faithfulness, Jephthah fulfills his vow. After allowing his daughter two months to mourn, Jephthah gives his daughter's life to the Lord. In his (and his daughter's) obedience, the warrior places God above his personal interests. As awful as it is, his actions boldly declare: Faithfulness to the Lord always costs something, and the one who is not willing to turn his back on his own family can never be a disciple.

Now your savvy pilgrim is bound to question the "faithfulness" of Jephthah's actions. For isn't the sacrifice of children an abomination to the Lord? Does it not break God's law? Further, he might even question the love of a God who would allow such an atrocity. How could a compassionate God expect Jephthah to be obedient to the point of sacrificing his only child?

But then you must remind your pilgrim, beloved Barnabas, of a God who did not spare His only Son, but gave Him as a ransom for many. What is more, you must recall to his memory the truth we've previously discussed in the life of

Samson. Namely, sin, even a foolish vow goaded by the devil, has consequences. Weren't Adam and Eve ejected from the Garden for their recklessness? And though God may forgive men's foolishness, it does not mean the consequences for sin do not remain.

God's chosen leaders are not immune from this reality. Indeed, the consequences they bear for their sin often serve best to educate all who follow in their footsteps. Samson was bound and blinded for his unbridled passion; King David watched his illegitimate son die and another son usurp his throne as a result of murdering Uriah and seducing Bathsheba; and the insubordinate prophet, Jonah, was thrown overboard into a raging sea. Though our Lord forgives and redeems each of these men, He allows His punishment on their sin to remain.

In a similar fashion, Jephthah reaps the consequences of his momentary collusion with the devil. God uses Jephthah's life as an example so the people of Israel may not repeat his folly. Hence the custom among the Israelites that each year the young women go out for four days to commemorate the daughter of Jephthah and the symbolism of her sacrifice.

From these events, dear Barnabas, I hope you will find sufficient means for the continued refinement of your pilgrim's heart. Help him see his wounds as a source of divine power, rather than a nidus of bitterness and resentment. Like Jephthah, help your man step forward in faith, away from the pains of his past toward the victories of the future. And as he progresses in this way, may your pilgrim seek peace. At the same time, however, may he always be prepared for war when God's way is obstructed.

Finally, with Jephthah's folly constantly in mind, cause your pilgrim to remember the gravity of a vow made before God. For even the rebellious prophet Jonah understood: "What I have vowed I will make good." As a result, your man should avoid vows before our Lord. Let his "Yes" be "Yes," and his "No," "No." But if he does vow, make sure he makes good on that vow!

May God Himself, the God of peace, sanctify your man through and through. May his whole spirit, soul, and body be kept blameless at the coming of our Lord Jesus Christ. The One who calls your pilgrim is faithful and He will do it! Until then, beloved Barnabas, do not grow weary in doing good.

Affectionately yours,
Uriel

# Letter 22

Beloved Barnabas,

In my previous correspondence, we were discussing the immortal folly of Jephthah. How my spirit still aches to recall his tragedy! But I trust Jephthah's rashness has made an indelible impression on your pilgrim. From what you report, it appears to have done so. What is more, I hope your man is amazed that even someone as marginalized, flawed, and apparently foolish as Jephthah, can nonetheless be redeemed by God into the hallowed halls of faith.

But if Jephthah's life fails to move your man's spiritual needle, then surely David's will. For it might be argued that the follies of David's life, and the sins he commits against God, are among the most storied in human history. And yet, our cousin David is described by the Lord as a man after God's own heart. The youngest son of Jesse is hand-picked by our King, anointed by His oil, and blessed to become the dynastic father of our Lord Jesus Christ. David's life of faith is a couplet of contraries from which your pilgrim might learn a great deal.

The first couplet to explore is favor and disfavor. David is honored by God from the moment of his calling. When the prophet Samuel is directed by the Lord to anoint the next king of Israel, God's selection does not fall on the likely older brother, Eliab. Indeed, Samuel is told to pass on all the brothers until none are left but the youngest, David, who is off tending sheep. This ruddy boy is then called and anointed with the power of the Spirit.

This anointing is then followed by the special favor of God. David is given the strength to kill the giant, Goliath, and destroy his enemies, the Philistines, in battle. Men from across the country then flock to David, drawn by the power of the Spirit of God within him. David's victories also win the hearts of Israel's common people. They sing about his exploits. Most of all, God commends David as a man after His own heart.

But of course, with the special favor of God comes the balance of the couplet: the animosity of our enemy. We see this same principle in the life of Job. God's blessing brings Satan's hatred. And as a result of blacklisting by the devil, David also incurs the disfavor of all those men still caught in the clutches of the Darkness.

David becomes the victim of King Saul's jealously and unbridled rage. The anointed son of Jesse is hunted like an animal and persecuted for years. He is forced to hide in caves and flee the country to escape the violent disfavor of Saul. Only upon the death of Saul does David dare to return to his country to assume the role God is grooming him for—the king of Israel.

With these events in mind, your pilgrim must understand the direct relationship between the favor of God and disfavor of the Darkness. To be anointed of Heaven means your man will be targeted by our enemy. He will be chased, hunted, and attacked just as David was. For if the Son of God was persecuted, will His disciples be spared?

But through it all, your pilgrim must look to David's example to see a disciple of faith who persists in God's grace. David clings to the Lord amidst his persecution. The son of Jesse recognizes God as his fortress and hiding place; and as a result, God sustains him. The anointed king says, "Surely God is my help, the Lord is the one who sustains me." Likewise, when your pilgrim clings to the Lord, God will sustain him no matter what devilry our enemy schemes.

Secondly, dear Barnabas, note the couplet of celebration and sadness throughout the life of David. For as his life testifies, the journey of faith will always have moments of praise and others of mourning. David dances and sings with gusto before the Lord as the young king welcomes the ark into Jerusalem. But does he not have reason to rejoice? God has finally come to His promised resting place! So David says, "I will praise you, O Lord, with all my heart;

141

I will tell of all your wonders. I will celebrate and rejoice in you; I will sing praise to your name, O Most High."

But this same celebratory king, as an older man, is forced to separate from the ark's presence. He is driven from Jerusalem by his conspiring son, Absalom. In sadness, shame and humiliation, David flees amidst the stoning and cursing of men like Shimei.

Though David's soul mourns God's chastisement, however, he never forgets that God is with him. David is convinced: Even though he passes through the valley of the shadow of death, the Lord will never leave him or forsake him. The king of Israel is confident that God can, and will, turn his mourning into dancing again!

Stress this fearless perspective to your fumbling pilgrim, beloved Barnabas. For every life of faith will encounter mountaintops and valleys. And though the pilgrim longs for the vision of the rocky summits, the mettle of his faith is proved and refined in the tangled valleys. The pilgrim who persists in faith through the sloughs of despond these valleys hold, however, will soon find reason to praise again. For the one who mourns shall be comforted. The one who persists shall be rewarded!

Finally, beloved Barnabas, we cannot conclude our reminiscing of David's life of faith without drawing your pilgrim's attention to the couplet of humility and pride. For the interplay between these two forces define David's journey of faith. The interaction between them produces some of the most spiritually vulnerable (and as a result, accessible) passages of Scripture. Many of the verses your man returns to emerge from David's inner battle with pride.

David's journey of faith begins in relative obscurity and humility. He is the youngest son of a shepherd. He grows up slinging stones rather than wearing armor and wielding a sword like his counterpart and future fast friend, Jonathan. David is a boy who, even after God's favor falls upon him, is able to say as a man, "Who am I?"

But eventually, the successes God bestows on David catch up with him. He begins to view himself as set apart, not only from other men, but also from the searching eyes of the God who has blessed him. So ensue the great follies of David's life. He premeditates, plots and orders the murder of his faithful servant, Uriah, after the wayward king seduces the warrior's wife. Later, David arrogantly orders a census of his army's might against the counsel of his advisors. Caught up in his power, David momentarily loses sight of the humble shepherd boy God favored to become king of Israel.

This lapse in spiritual discernment, however, proves the fertile ground for God's instruction. The Lord's chastisement of David's sins brings repentance. And with it, David's return to humility. For the king recognizes our Lord desires a broken and contrite heart above all else. Unless a man—even the king of Israel—comes to the Lord like a little child, he will never enter the Kingdom. In this humble awareness, the Spirit then pens through David some of the world's most beloved verse.

As your pilgrim manages his own constant battle between pride and humility, bring him back to David's experience. Remind him that God is close to the brokenhearted, but opposes the proud. Cause him to recall how our Lord loves to turn mourning into dancing for the one who persists in faith. Make every effort to keep your man's heart broken and contrite before the Lord!

Similarly, dear Barnabas, focus your pilgrim's attention of the duality of God's favor and Satan's animus. Bring to his awareness the direct relationship between a growing proximity to our Father and the calculated attacks of our enemy. In light of this reality, strengthen your charge's resolve and his divine confidence. That is, impress upon him the truth that the One who is in him is far greater than the one who is in the world. And though the devil may beset him, Christ will not lose one of those whom have been entrusted to His care.

*Therefore, my brother, help your pilgrim to not be carried away by the error of lawless men and so fall from his secure position into a needlessly vulnerable one. Rather, assist him to grow in the grace and knowledge of our Lord and his Savior, Jesus Christ. To Him be the glory both now and forever more!*

*Affectionately yours,*

## Uriel

# Letter 23

Beloved Barnabas,

My longing to see you face to face, my brother, is tempered only by my immense pleasure in the fruit of the Spirit's work through you. For I note your pilgrim's recent identification with David's flawed humanity; and I delight in your man's subsequent brokenness before God. With this contrite heart, he is now more fully prepared for the challenges of the remaining journey ahead.

As we have seen, David's life on earth was also full of challenges. But by God's grace, those challenges refined a heart after God into an instrument of His glory. Perhaps no one had a better firsthand view of this divine work than our cousin, the prophet Samuel. And while David's life might instruct your pilgrim in the dualities of divine favor and disfavor, joy and sadness, and humility and pride, Samuel's life of faith might prove equally instructive. For the prophet's story showcases several other vital components of faith: legacy, dedication, spiritual receptivity, and tough love.

Let us begin by drawing your pilgrim's attention to the spiritual legacy Samuel inherits and the legacy he leaves. For every man inherits a spiritual legacy, just as he leaves one. His inherited legacy may be good or bad; over this the man has no direct control. And his spiritual inheritance may help root him in the Truth that saves him, or drive him into the Darkness that will consume him.

One thing an inherited legacy will never be, however, is unimportant or uninfluential. In one way or another, it contributes to shaping the soul. While God can (and sometimes does) create a totally new work in the heart of a man independent of legacy, more often than not, a man's spiritual inheritance is one of the components our Lord uses to mold the next generation of faith. An inherited legacy may be used by God to perfect a new legacy of faith.

Much like your pilgrim, the Samuel we have come to know so well is the product of a beautiful spiritual legacy. His mother, Hannah, is a devout and holy woman who even then, just as now, sought the Lord in the tenderness of her heart. But like many pilgrims, her heart knew great sadness while on earth. In her barrenness, her maternal instincts longed for a child. And in her pain, she was ridiculed and provoked by her rival.

Nonetheless, in the faithfulness of faith, Hannah presented her request to the Lord year after year. In the bitterness of her soul, she opened her broken heart before the Lord: "O Lord Almighty, if you will only look upon your servant's misery and remember me, and not

147

forget your servant but give her a son, then I will give him to the Lord all the days of his life." And because of her devotion, the Lord remembered Hannah. She gave birth to a son—Samuel.

The spiritual legacy of Samuel's life would have been incomplete and ineffectual at this point, however, without the further fulfillment of Hannah's promise. Therefore, after weaning the boy, Hannah returned to the house of the Lord in Shiloh and presented Samuel back to God. She was faithful to her promise. As a result, the Lord blessed her womb with many more children.

This example had a profound effect upon the young Samuel. Through the candid and emotionally vulnerable faith of his mother, Samuel meets a God who remembers His suffering children and answers the prayers of their hearts. Yahweh is not just an idea or concept, but a living God who hears the cries of the broken heart and moves mightily in the lives of His people. Such was Hannah's legacy to the young Samuel.

On this point, dear Barnabas, do not fail to exploit your educational opportunity. For like Samuel, your pilgrim is also the product of a rich spiritual legacy. Cause him to carefully consider this legacy in his family. For instance, draw the direct parallel to the prayers of his own mother, and the faithfulness of our Lord in providing for all her needs. In this way, your pilgrim might be encouraged to recall the power of prayer, the love of God, and the ensuing faithfulness of Heaven.

Through the outworking of this same divine faithfulness, Hannah made good on her promise to God: she dedicated Samuel to the Lord. For his whole life, Samuel was given over to God's service. From boyhood till death, he ministered before the Lord and His people. In faith, he worshipped the Lord. As a result, Samuel's spiritual legacy lives on in the immortality of Scripture.

In an effort to build his or her own legacy of faith, every disciple must commit to a similar divine dedication. A man may not be called to the priesthood, but he is, nonetheless, a "priest" in the service of the Lord. For when a life like Samuel's is given to God, the whole life must follow. Our Lord has said, "No one who puts his hand to the plow and looks back is fit for service in the Kingdom of God." Once dedicated, Samuel did not look back. He faithfully walked forward in the service of Heaven.

But again, though Samuel's life on earth was exemplary, his dedication to God should not be seen as some isolated and anomalous example. Indeed, quite the contrary! Every man and woman, including your pilgrim, who is born again—baptized and resurrected in the power of the Spirit—has a life dedicated to God. Therefore, from his spiritual childhood onward, the disciple's life is called to be a living sacrifice to his heavenly Father. The pilgrim who places his hand to the plow and longingly looks back to the world he has left is not fit for the service of the Kingdom.

This dedicated life will also be marked by a spiritual sensitivity and receptivity. For even as a boy, Samuel's heart was attuned to the Lord's Spirit. As you may recall, Barnabas, one night the young Samuel was lying down in the temple of the Lord. Our Father called to Samuel, and Samuel heard His voice. Eli, the priest and God's appointed minister, did not hear God speaking. But Samuel did. For his life was dedicated to God; and as a result, his heart was touched by the Spirit.

With this divine touch, Samuel received the communication of God. The favor of the Lord came upon Samuel, and none of the young boy's words fell to ground. Because he feared the Lord, God shared His heart with Samuel.

Every true disciple who pilgrims toward Heaven must desire to emulate a similar spiritual sensitivity and receptivity. His heart must be open to hear the Spirit's calls. On the other side of the coin, the closed heart will have ears that do not hear and a heart that does not understand. Like the wicked sons of Eli and the Pharisees denounced by Jesus, their hearts will not receive the Lord's communication or favor because they are sealed off in their false religiosity. Make sure, dear Barnabas, your pilgrim always maintains the humble and contrite spirit capable of hearing God's voice and receiving His instruction. Even if you have to rough him up a bit, Barnabas, keep that heart tender!

In this spirit, Samuel's life of faith finally demonstrates for your pilgrim the necessity for tough love. Time and time again, Samuel's righteous life butted up against the iniquity and disobedience of Israel and her leaders. Samuel the boy divulged to Eli the hard truth concerning God's condemnation of Eli's sons. The boy held nothing back. Samuel the prophet implored the people to put away their Baals and Ashtorehs and serve the Lord, before heading out to war against the Philistines. And Samuel the priest of God, confronted and condemned Israel's king, Saul, after the leader's disobedience to God's commands.

In every instance, Samuel dared to love his brother enough to correct him. For tough love—the love of Heaven—does not allow a sinner to go on wandering. This love confronts, rebukes as necessary, and gently corrects in an effort to save the lost from death and cover a multitude of sins.

Samuel never demurred in God's service of tough love. In the exercise of this love, his life of faith continues to demonstrate the power of spiritual legacy, the necessity for dedication of heart, and the importance of spiritual receptivity. Use all these reminders, my brother, to continue your work of grace in the life of your pilgrim. And by that grace, may your man be equipped with everything he needs to devote himself to doing Heaven's work.

Until I am caused to write again, dear Barnabas, may the love of our Father rest upon you.

Affectionately yours,
Uriel

# Letter 24

Beloved Barnabas,

How are you holding up my brother? I hear the weariness in your most recent letter. And it's quite understandable. For without a doubt, your current mission has been a relentless one. In fact, Gabriel and I were just discussing your tireless efforts on behalf of your unruly pilgrim.

But as our cousin Paul so aptly reminded the Corinthians, do not lose heart. For though your pilgrim has made you work for every inch of ground in the rocky soil of his soul, the Spirit who empowers your efforts promises to renew your strength day by day. The light and momentary affliction you are now enduring is helping achieve for your pilgrim an eternal weight of glory beyond comparison.

This is the same glory by which we live and move and have our being. Our solemn duty is to help bring the pilgrim's awareness to his dependence upon this Glory. For God's glory is His goodness, and His goodness comes to all those who earnestly seek Him. Therefore, as you continue your labor of love for your pilgrim's sanctification, may your struggles inform your ministry. Impress upon your man's heart the weight of glory his sanctification is achieving.

153

And so, by all means, spur him onward in his journey of faith.

Since the dawn of God's creation, few disciples of faith have had a better grasp of God's incomprehensible glory than the prophets. Some of them, like Moses and Isaiah, even had mortal lives blessed with glimpses of that Glory. And what Isaiah saw caused him to exclaim, "Woe is me! I am ruined!"

But in His grace, God spared Isaiah, just as He did Moses and every other prophet who glimpsed the fringes of His glory. However, with this mercy came the compelling commission of faith. For a true disciple can never have an encounter with God and remain unchanged. He can never feel the Father's love and not, at the same time, appreciate the tremendous debt of love he owes to Love. So the disciple's life becomes a willing instrument in the hands of Heaven.

Again, take for example the prophet Isaiah. He was called to go to the Lord's people and preach His two-pronged message of judgement on sin and salvation through the coming Messiah. In faith, Isaiah responded to the Lord: "Here I am, send me!" His life became a sword of truth and an oracle of hope.

Or perhaps Jeremiah: He never wanted to be a prophet in the first place. Indeed, he told the Lord he did not know how to speak; he was only a child. But when God touched his lips,

Jeremiah's faith was changed. He became a prophet who boldly confronted kings and priests with a message of imminent doom and future hope. His faith endured tears and persecution alike, because Jeremiah knew the Lord was with him like a mighty warrior.

And how about Ezekiel? God required Ezekiel's life to become a living portent for the nation of Israel. The Lord took from Ezekiel the delight of his eyes, his wife's life, and then told the prophet not to shed a tear. Was God asking his heart of flesh to become a heart of stone? Didn't the Lord promise the exact opposite? Why make Ezekiel suffer in this way? Was it not so the nation of Israel might vividly understand the impending desecration of the Lord's sanctuary? What faith Ezekiel had! Few men possess it.

Of course, we could go on at length examining the lives of faith demonstrated by the other prophets: Amos, the shepherd called to confront Jeroboam, king of Israel; Zechariah, the priest who boldly prophesized during the days of Darius; Nahum, the voice of judgement against Assyria, and so forth. But as it pertains to your pilgrim's journey of faith, I believe a closer look at the lives of Jonah, Hosea and Daniel will be particularly instructive. Each of these prophets, in their weaknesses and strengths alike, have specific points of connection for your pilgrim's heart.

155

So let's begin by turning our attention to the life of Jonah. Now at first blush, Jonah's journey of faith might not strike your pilgrim as commendable. Indeed, Jonah was surly, selfish and blinded by his own self-righteousness. Yet because he was guilty of all of these things, God's work through him still speaks loudly. For there is a bit of Jonah in every man, including your pilgrim. But importantly, despite all of Jonah's flaws, God still chose him as Heaven's instrument of salvation to the city of Ninevah. Why?

The answer to this question is in part due to Jonah's universality. That is, the everyman in Jonah, and the Jonah in every man. For Jonah's first response to God's command was much like many: avoidance. Your man, Barnabas, has been guilty of this many times. But when the Lord told Jonah to go to Ninevah and preach against the city's wickedness, the prophet went one step further. He ran the other way!

No doubt there is something refreshingly honest about this response. You have to chuckle at the audacity! Can you imagine trying to run from God? But has your man not desired to do the same? Has his spirit not bucked at the reins and champed at the bit? And yet, in his weakness, how often he has tried instead to quietly deny his sedition and subtly hide his treachery. Jonah, however, had the temerity to flee. He boarded a ship for Tarshish. He openly rebelled. But here's the thing: As it pertains to baseline intention, is your man's contemplation of desertion really all that different than Jonah's boarding of the ship? Cause your man to ponder that question.

With this thought in mind, pause to impress upon your pilgrim the following axiom: The journey of faith will always have a harbor full of ships ready to sail to Tarshish. There will be no lack of opportunities to run from God's mission. And the Lord will not prevent your man from boarding one of those ships, any more than he precluded Jonah's bullheaded efforts.

Though your pilgrim may be given the freedom to book his passage, however, make sure he does so with his eyes wide open. For Jonah's example demonstrates the futility of running from God. When it comes to the Lord's chosen people, flight does not bring the felicity of halcyon seas, but the ferocity of God's storms.

Of course you and I know, Barnabas, that the Lord's unrelenting love ultimately powers these storms. Because our Lord is a Father who adores His children, He sends the winds and the waves in pursuit of them. Even if a man decides to settle on the far side of the sea, even there God's hand will find him. For there is no place to hide from His presence.

Deep down inside, even the fleeing Jonah knew this truth. In proof of fact, when the sailors

157

singled him out, Jonah readily admitted his responsibility for the foul weather. He told the men to throw him overboard. Jonah knew the Lord was pursuing him, even on the high seas.

In this moment, the prophet's honesty took a turn for the better. Rather than denying culpability, Jonah claimed it. Instead of avoiding his call to righteousness, Jonah embraced it. He willing became the sacrifice that calmed the sea. Because his faith—however irascible and reluctant it might have been—still feared God, the sailors were drawn to fear the Lord as well. When the men saw the ocean calm as it swallowed Jonah, they sacrificed to the Lord of Heaven and earth. To top it all off (in perhaps one of the Author's greatest twists of plot!), Jonah unwittingly prefigured the future death and resurrection of our Lord. The surly prophet became the symbol for Christ's ultimate victory! Isn't our Lord marvelous!

Now in the midst of the raging seas, Jonah could never have imagined his resurrection would involve a giant fish swallowing him. That he might spend three days in the belly of that monster, only to be coughed up on the shore to resume his mission, would have been even more unimaginable. But I don't have to tell you, Barnabas, that is just how our Lord works—in unimaginable ways! His mercy often moves in the cloak of the storm, on the brink of death, and in the grasp of the depths. Love moves in mysterious ways. Let your pilgrim look to Jonah's example to see a God whose love is not bound by natural laws.

In the mystery of his own moment, Jonah prayed from inside the fish. And by grace, his faith hung on. Though he was banished, Jonah remained confident that he would look on the Lord's temple again. Though he had been thrown into the depths, his faith believed he would see the salvation of the Lord. Jonah promised to make good on his vow.

Despite his renewed perspective, however, it didn't take Jonah long to fall back into his old habits. The prophet obeyed God and delivered the Lord's message to the people of Ninevah. But when they heard it, they repented. As a result, God averted His anger from them. And seeing this mercy, Jonah slid back into his surly self-righteousness. The prophet even had the audacity to use God's compassion towards Ninevah as justification for his prior disobedience. Jonah was so angry he asked God to take away his life. What a churlish and ungrateful brat!

Granted, however, it's easy for you and me, Barnabas, to see the childishness of Jonah's response. Because we fear God, we easily understand our Lord is always right—even when the justice we think appropriate gives way to the mercy we might think too extravagant. We have the humility to admit we are not God, and in His wisdom, God knows best.

But men like Jonah sometimes fall prey to their flawed and myopic vision. They become miniature providences in their own eyes. As a result, each man does what he sees fit to do. Of course, you know where that leads. You'll remember the time of the judges where this distorted mentality ran rampant. At moments, it was absolute moral chaos! Recall that poor concubine from Bethlehem, Barnabas? How she was chopped up by her husband and delivered to the twelve tribes? Awful stuff!

Nonetheless, your pilgrim must be led to identify this same despicable propensity in his own heart. For Jonah's selfishness is not unique. And you and I have both observed a similar small-minded pettiness in your pilgrim—the griping, kvetching, and accusing—all of which question his fear of the Lord.

Therefore, make a point, my brother, of drawing your man's conscience to his own self-righteousness. Help him to extract the plank out of his own eye before he is drawn to expose the speck in the eye of another. At all times, encourage in him a graciousness of spirit that recognizes the undeserved mercy he has received. For was he not also saved from the sea of sin he found himself flailing in? Has he not been resurrected from the depths?

Finally, do not fail to extract one further witness from Jonah's example: The journey of faith is a work in progress. Justification couldn't be any more simple; it's a gift. Sanctification, however, is an ongoing battle. Holiness is anything but a linear journey. It's a messy, slow slog, plagued by the tendency for recidivism. The life of Jonah and the history of Israel both attest to this reality.

As your pilgrim struggles with his own tendency for backsliding, may his heart find encouragement in these biblical examples of imperfection. For though Jonah was a prophet during his time on earth, he was as deeply flawed as any other man. In the ebb and flow of his imperfect faith, however, the unfathomable mercy and love of our God emerge victorious. So too with the people of Israel. Though their faithfulness has waxed and waned, God's love for them, and His plans to give them hope and a future, persist to this day.

This truth notwithstanding, make your pilgrim aware, my brother, that these promises come to the one who seeks the Lord with all his heart. Though your man's journey may be an imperfect one—bedeviled by days of doubt, frustration and self-inflicted dejection—if by faith your pilgrim persists in his pursuit of God, your man will find the King. If your pilgrim is captive to some demon, he can be brought back into the arms of love; if he has been swallowed by some monster in the sea of sin, he might be spit up on a new shore, readied for mission. If only he pursues the Lord as the deer pants for streams of water!

The pursuit of holiness is the dogged journey of faith. But as Jonah's example so clearly illustrates, the grace of God is able to redeem even the most reluctant pilgrimages. As a result, do not fail, dear Barnabas, to expose the inner Jonah lurking in the heart of your man and encourage his lackluster efforts.

At the same time, use the prophet's example to reveal the tenacity of God's love for man—how He relentlessly and recklessly pursues His chosen ones, even with the wind, the waves, and the monsters of the deep. May your pilgrim know that He who watches over Israel, watches over him. The Lord will be the shade at your man's right hand, so the sun will not harm him by day, nor the moon at night. For the Lord is watching over his life, his coming and his going, both now and forevermore.

Now may the peace of God that calms even the fiercest wind and waves, rest upon you and your tireless work, beloved Barnabas.

Affectionately yours,
Uriel

# Letter 25

*Beloved Barnabas,*

*I note your pilgrim's recent heartening in regards to God's pursuit of Jonah. Interesting—isn't it?—how it is often our Father's work in the most lackluster souls that brings the greatest effect. Perhaps the dark backdrop of their unremarkable faith provides the best contrast for our Lord's radiance. I believe their painters have a term for this in art—chiaroscuro, if I'm not mistaken. It means "light-dark," or the technique by which the fullness of the subject is visually achieved through tonal contrasts. Obviously, they've learned from the Master! He's been doing this since the dawn of creation.*

*In any event, if your pilgrim has found encouragement in God's pursuit of Jonah, then he may be all the more encouraged by the life of faith evinced in the prophet Hosea. For Hosea's story is an extended allegory of the Lord's love for the wayward and lost. In faith, Hosea finds himself called by God to emulate the love of the Lord: that reckless, relentless affection that dares to love the unfaithful and the unlovable.*

*To illustrate the depth of this divine affection, God calls Hosea to take the prostitute, Gomer, as his wife. The Lord refers to her as an* "adulterous" woman and the offspring she bears as "children of unfaithfulness." In their very names, they represent the people of Israel and their broken relationship with God. The ill-repute of their physical lives embodies the spiritual dissonance of God's chosen people.

With this symbolism in mind, the Lord works in and through Hosea's faith. When his wife, Gomer, is unfaithful, the Lord tells Hosea to take her back. Instead of divorcing her for her infidelity, or allowing her to be stoned for her adulterous behavior as the Mosaic law would allow, Hosea is called by God to love her! He is called to forgive her blatant indiscretions and to bring her back into his dwelling. No easy task! For betrayal is one of the hardest things to forgive. Yet that is entirely God's point.

Through Hosea, the Lord is illustrating His unreasonable love for the nation of Israel, a people who have betrayed Him time and time again. But then love, if it is true—as God's love always is—is by nature unreasonable. If it is perfectly predictable, always logical, and never surprises with its magnanimity, then it is not love. Certainly not God's love!

As you know so well, however, even the best and purest human love pales in comparison. For without the Spirit, man's love is a flawed facsimile. In light of this sobering reality, cause your pilgrim, dear Barnabas, to place himself in

Hosea's shoes. How might the prophet have felt after his wife's transgressions? Help your pilgrim to imagine the hurt and humiliation Hosea processed when his wife brazenly embraced other lovers.

In this contemplation, your man might then be induced to consider how our Lord felt about the nation of Israel (and still feels for the world at large!)—the humiliation, shame, and brokenness of heart our Father endured as His chosen people bowed before a host of foreign gods. How they happily exchanged their Glory for something disgraceful. For though the Lord led them with cords of human kindness; though He fed them until they were satisfied; though He protected them from their enemies; even so, His people trusted in their own strength. They became proud, self-reliant and promiscuous. And yet, our Father loved them still. Talk about enduring unfaithfulness! What our Lord has put up with is unfathomable, isn't it?

Even today, however, despite Israel's ongoing infidelity, the Lord is as unwilling to give up on His people now as He was in the days of Hosea. Like the prophet called to love the unfaithful wife, God gives His people an undeserved love. Your pilgrim is a recipient of this love too! Make sure he never forgets this, dear Barnabas.

Through Hosea's example, the Lord stresses not only His unfathomable love for man, but also man's call to love one another. For did our Lord not command His disciples to love one another as He has loved them? Use Hosea's story, dear Barnabas, to demonstrate for your pilgrim the kind of love our Lord calls men to embrace in their relationships with one another—the unreasonable, at times nonsensical, and certainly extravagant love of Heaven: the kind of love the Good Samaritan also illustrates. For unless a man loves with God's love, he does not love at all.

Secondly, draw your pilgrim's attention to the unflagging pursuit of this heavenly love. Indeed, Hosea's story is one of many that might be used to impress upon your pilgrim the relentless nature of God's love for His people. Though they are, like Gomer, persistently unfaithful, God is avid in His pursuit of them. And because of His avidity to save the hearts of men, His people are called to embrace the same tireless pursuit for the lost. The true disciple pursues as God pursues—relentlessly.

Finally, Hosea's example of faith evinces the language of forgiveness so vital to God's narrative. Hosea is called to forgive his unfaithful wife without reservation. He is asked to extend to her undeserved mercy and grace. Why? Because God has shown Hosea, and every other pilgrim like yours, a greater forgiveness—the ultimate one.

Therefore, use Hosea's example, Barnabas, to illustrate our Lord's words when He gives His disciples the forgiveness imperative: "For if you forgive men when they sin against you, your heavenly Father will also forgive you. But if you do not forgive men their sins, your Father will not forgive your sins." Unless your pilgrim is willing, like Hosea, to forgive the unforgivable in others, God will not forgive him. Indeed, the life of faith understands forgiveness is contingent upon forgiveness. There are no exceptions!

The pilgrim who embraces these lessons of faith will be ransomed from the power of the grave and redeemed from death. The sinner who returns to God and maintains love and justice, waiting for God always, will find the salvation of the Lord. For the ways of the Lord are right, and the righteous walk in them.

With this truth in mind, continue to faithfully guide your pilgrim on the road to Heaven, dear Barnabas. Though your man may stumble, he will not fall. For the Lord's love will support him as God's hands work through you to hold him fast.

Affectionately yours,

Uriel

# Letter 26

*Beloved Barnabas,*

*I left off my last letter exhorting you to harness the confidence of Heaven in your soul-shaping work. For as you're aware, my brother, the Spirit works in and through you to achieve His divine purposes. As a result, all your efforts ought to be accompanied by a quiet confidence. For God's gentleness operates through you, and His purposes never fail. Rest assured—you're an instrument of victory! And my hope is that your pilgrim will catch the contagion of this heavenly contentment as you help minister to his faith.*

*Rooted in this hope, you will do well, Barnabas, to remember how few men of faith demonstrate the gentle power of heavenly confidence better than the prophet Daniel. In fact, his life on earth was a constant reminder of how God works through a man of faith to accomplish Heaven's agendas: with a slow, steady and unstoppable force. The Lord's work in a righteous man is a mighty river that always reaches God's determined end.*

*In Daniel's life, this divine work played out along the banks of the mighty Euphrates River. As you no doubt remember, Daniel and the people of Israel were taken captive by King Nebuchadnezzar and led to that great city of sin,*

Babylon. And there, by the king's order, Daniel and his godly peers were conscripted into the service of the Babylonian Empire.

As a man of faith, however, Daniel always served the Lord. Though his position on earth answered to King Nebuchadnezzar, his position in Heaven made him accountable to God. Though Nebuchadnezzar had to learn this lordship lesson the hard way, Daniel knew it instinctively. And he never forgot it!

From the beginning of his exile, Daniel demonstrated the determined confidence of a true man of faith. When the king's servant wanted to place Daniel and his peers on a diet that would have defiled them before the Lord, Daniel resolved that he would not sin. But how would he resist the king's order? No one disobeyed Nebuchadnezzar and lived.

Daniel feared the Lord more than the king of Babylon, however. So the young Israelite devised a plan: a ten day dietary test—vegetables and water versus the royal food and wine. Daniel knew God would honor his commitment to Heaven by giving him success. And so the Lord did! By faith, Daniel and his peers outshone the men who ate the royal food.

This same determination of faith marked Daniel's entire tenure under the kings of Babylon and Persia. Rooted in a holy fear of God, Daniel's faith exhibited a quiet confidence. But no less

169

important for your pilgrim is the example of spiritual discipline Daniel's life of faith presents. For even in the midst of exile and spiritual hostility, Daniel remained true to the disciplines of faith. Whether it was dietary restrictions or the practice of daily prayer, Daniel never gave up on the disciplines of faith.

Importantly, however, Daniel did not worship those disciplines. He did not—as the Pharisees after him would be guilty of—become a hypocritical devotee of the rituals themselves. Rather, Daniel recognized those disciplines as essential components of his obedience and fidelity to the true King.

With Daniel's example, therefore, make this point clear to your pilgrim: No man of faith arrives at the gates of Heaven without spiritual discipline. Indeed, it's an oxymoron to speak of an undisciplined spiritual life. For faith requires discipline or it dies. And while the individual disciplines that help prune the life of faith should neither be demonized nor deified, they should be employed as tools to keep the heart on track.

Daniel demonstrated this God-pleasing balance. Indeed, he did it so well our Lord esteemed him. But not without reason. For recall if you will, Barnabas, how under the reign of Darius the Mede, Daniel's disciplined faith was put the ultimate test. The envious royal administrators induced Darius to decree punishment on anyone who prayed to any god or man other than the king: that man should be thrown into the lion's den.

What did Daniel do when he learned of this decree? Did he bow down and pray to Darius? Did he cease his daily discipline of prayer to the God of Heaven and earth? By no means! Indeed, as soon as Daniel learned of the decree, he went home and prayed. He did what he always did— bowed down before the King of Heaven. In the discipline of faith, he remained faithful.

Of course as you know, Barnabas, this holy resistance was not without effect. For through it, God gained the opportunity to bring glory to His name! Daniel was quickly arrested by the authorities and thrown into the lion's den. Then, by our Lord's decree, our brother was sent into the den to shut the mouths of the lions. The beasts did not even touch Daniel. His faith rescued him. And in joy, Darius declared that all people of his kingdom should fear and reverence the God of Daniel!

Much more could be said, dear Barnabas, about Daniel's example of faith: How the Spirit filled him with unearthly wisdom; how Daniel interpreted dreams and prophesized the future, even the last days; how he committed to intercessory prayer on behalf of his people; and how he spoke with our Lord, who commended Daniel's desire to gain understanding and humble himself before the King of Heaven. Yes, Daniel's life of faith still speaks loudly! And while we could go on at length recounting the countless other episodes of Daniel's remarkable faith journey, it will have to wait till another time.

For the time being, therefore, make good use of the narrative we've already discussed, my brother. Stress the quiet confidence of the Spirit that steadied Daniel's faith in exile. For because Daniel was filled with the Spirit, he walked amongst fearsome kings and beasts alike, unafraid. Daniel did not fear because he was filled with the Fear of Heaven.

As we have also seen, Daniel's walk of faith was further ballasted by his spiritual disciplines. He treated his body as a temple of the Spirit, committed himself to daily prayer, and read Scripture regularly. He did not fail to exercise his faith like a muscle. As a result, God honored him with the strength he needed to run his race.

Help situate your pilgrim's thinking in the same way, dear Barnabas. For he too is running his race of faith. Assist him in throwing off everything that hinders and the sin that so easily entangles, and exhort him to run with perseverance the remaining race marked out for him. Encourage him to run with the full expectation of receiving the prize. But remind him: The victory crown goes to those who, like Daniel, have committed themselves to the demanding disciplines of faith. For the undisciplined faith will fail as surely as the untrained athlete. And finally, make sure your charge never forgets: God's grace is with him to the very end! So let him fix his eyes on Jesus.

With these words I'll leave you to it, dear Barnabas. Let Daniel's faith inspire your man to better things! And may the Author and Perfecter of faith continue His refining work through your loving ministrations.

Affectionately yours,
*Uriel*

# Letter 27

*Beloved Barnabas,*

*Our angelic congregation notes with pleasure the renewed discipline of your pilgrim's spiritual life. More importantly, however, we delight in how this discipline is enabling your man to tap into the grace and power of our Lord. For Christ is the Vine that sustains your man. And with your man's deepening connection with this Source of life, your pilgrim is growing in the confidence of the Spirit. He is the Witness who enables men to stand unscathed in the presence of lions and walk untouched through the flames.*

*As we have seen, Daniel was a man of faith filled with the Spirit. But of equal merit for the training of your pilgrim is the faith exhibited by Daniel's close contemporaries: Hananiah, Mishael and Azariah; or, as the Babylonians renamed them, Shadrach, Meshach, and Abednego. These three men are still remembered for their bold declaration of loyalty to our Father. Even in the face of flames, they refused to recant.*

*You no doubt remember the details of their story, dear Barnabas: How that arrogant and insolent King Nebuchadnezzar erected a golden image on the plain of Dura; how he demanded all peoples to bow before that image of gold; and how* he threatened to throw the disobedient into the fiery furnace.

But Shadrach, Meshach and Abednego refused to bow. For what Nebuchadnezzar failed to consider was the heart of the faithful. When a man or woman is filled with the Spirit, then the Presence of God lives in him. And of course, God will not—cannot—bow to any other competing god!

As men will do, however, Nebuchadnezzar attempted to live in his fantasy world. He tried to get the Lord of Heaven to bow before him. Can you imagine? The delusions of these men know no bounds! They truly are remarkable creatures, are they not?

In any event, the madman who declared Babylon was created by his power for his glory, believed himself equal to God. So in an effort to exert his will, the king threatened, and then delivered, his punishment on the three young Jews. They were thrown into the fire. But not before they declared with confidence the power of God to save them and the great "Even if..." of faith! Collectively they said to king:

> If we are thrown into the blazing furnace, the God we serve is able to save us from it, and He will rescue us from your hand. But even if He does not, we want you to know,

175

O king, that we will not serve your gods or worship the image of gold you have set up.

There is perhaps no greater testament of faith than this declaration. It exerts the confidence of the heavenly man and the loyalty of the redeemed heart. It testifies to God's ability to save, as well as the disciples' acceptance of the Lord's sovereignty over all things. For true faith requires both: divine confidence and infinite resignation. It is the life that declares: God can and I willingly accept! The former provides the strength to win, and the latter expresses the necessary humility to fall in behind the Victor.

This faith recognizes God is stronger and He knows better. It graciously concedes God gives men what they need, not what they necessarily want. When a pilgrim like yours, Barnabas, is equipped with these spiritual perspectives, no fire will consume him!

Shadrach, Meshach and Abednego set the example. Because of their faith, our Lord met them in the furnace. Importantly, however, He did not keep the Jews <u>from</u> the fire, but delivered them <u>through</u> the flames. Make sure to stress this point to your pilgrim, dear Barnabas. For many pilgrims of faith live under the illusion that they should not have to face fiery trials; that a good God should spare them from entering the furnace in the first place.

The courageous example set by Daniel's companions proves otherwise, however. For they felt the heat of the furnace, stoked seven times hotter than usual. They physically fell into the fire. And yet, they were not burned or even singed. They did not smell of smoke. Though the flames killed the guards, the three Jews joined our Lord as He walked freely amidst the flames.

Therefore, your pilgrim must remember: God does not promise the absence of fire, but the grace to walk through the flames. His goodness lies not in forgoing the furnace, but in the purification its heat brings. For everything of value must be purified. The soul of the pilgrim is no exception. Tough as it may be, make sure your man never forgets this axiom.

Additionally, draw your pilgrim's attention to the loyalty demonstrated by the three Jews during this process. The strength of their fealty to God testifies to their love of the Father. For most love is a fickle thing. It is often a fair weather phenomenon that vacillates according to the individual's benefit. But divine love never changes. It is willing to lose its life in the service of the one it loves. When a pilgrim is filled with this kind of love, he proceeds into the fire with resolution. And even if God chooses not to rescue him, the pilgrim remains confident that the God he loves is with him always.

With these thoughts in mind, dear Barnabas, use the example of Shadrach, Meshach and Abednego to strengthen the resolve of your man. Remind him that the God he serves is able to rescue him from the flames. He will meet him in the fire and walk with him. And when he is delivered from the furnace, it will be for the glory of the Most High God.

On this note, I return you and your attention to your heavenly service. Like our cousins in the fiery furnace, your loyalty to our Lord brings Him great delight. Only continue in the grace that sustains all things.

Affectionately yours,
## Uriel

# Letter 28

Beloved Barnabas,

I don't quite know how to interpret your most recent communication. Do you mean to tell me your man found the example of the three Jews in the flames a bit unnerving? Was he discouraged or encouraged? I guess both are possibilities in light of such an incredible display of faith. For the men's bold declaration is literally seared onto the pages of history. And the power of their words was, and still is, not without effect—to the glory of the Most High God. If you have done your work well, however, your man must be in awe of their courage, even if he feels—perhaps rightly so!—a bit under par.

Regardless of how your insecure man is feeling right now, however, the example of the three royal counselors confirms that the witness of faith demands testimony. It's important for your pilgrim to understand that this opportunity may come in a variety of forms and at unexpected times. For Shadrach, Meshach and Abednego, it came with the fiery furnace. Their climatic moment before Nebuchadnezzar proves how the testimony of faith requires both declaration and action. An effective witness not only testifies to God's grace, but also goes in that

179

grace wherever God's sovereignty takes it. To be a true disciple, your pilgrim must be ready to pick up his cross and go wherever the Spirit leads; and to endure whatever God requires of him.

As we have seen, sometimes our Lord rescues men from the fire to testify another day. The three Jews survived the furnace. Not a hair on their heads was singed. They did not even smell of smoke.

At other times, however, God's infinite wisdom and mercy may see best to promote the pilgrim to glory immediately after his testimony. Although rare, martyrdom may be required. So the true disciple must always be ready and willing for this sacrifice of faith. That's the "even if" of faith. For the one who loves is willing to die for his Love. What is your sense, Barnabas? Is your pilgrim ready? Is he willing?

The lives of the early apostles stress the reality of this commitment. As the Church's song, "Martyrs for the Lord," recounts: Matthew was stabbed to death in Persia; Mark and Thomas torn apart by horses; Luke cruelly hanged; Peter, Phillip and Simon crucified; Bartholomew skinned alive; James cut in half with a saw, and Matthias beheaded. And the list of the faithful who gave their lives for the Truth goes on. But of course, the first witness to be martyred for his faith in Christ was Stephen.

Recall if you will, dear Barnabas, the context of Stephen's historic testimony. The early Church was exploding with growth, and Stephen, along with a number of others, was chosen to minister among the widows. During his short ministry, he was a man full of God's grace and power. The Spirit worked miracles and wondrous signs through him and filled him with wisdom.

As a result, the power of Stephen's testimony made him a target for our enemy. For the brighter the Light shines into the shadows, the more the Darkness wants to extinguish it. So Stephen was seized by zealous men and falsely accused. But though the night closed in around him, his face shone with our angelic radiance. God's moment for Stephen had arrived.

Before the Sanhedrin, Stephen testified to God's grace, power and purpose in and through the people of Israel, from Abraham down to Jesus. With climatic emphasis he courageously addressed his accusers:

> You stiff-necked people, with uncircumcised hearts and ears! You are just like your fathers: You always resist the Holy Spirit! Was there ever a prophet your fathers did not persecute? They even killed those who predicted the coming of the Righteous One. And now you have

betrayed and murdered Him—you who have received the law that was put into effect through angels but have not obeyed it.

What a beautifully scorching reprimand, don't you agree Barnabas! We couldn't have done it better (he even references us!). For it strikes right to the heart of the matter—namely, that their hearts were closed and their ears were blocked. Such is the affliction of the unregenerate. And Stephen shone God's light on it.

This courageous illumination is God's will not only for Stephen, however, but also for every pilgrim, including your fumbling man. Indeed, no matter how stutteringly simple the man might be, his life is called to bear witness to God's grace, power and purpose. He is called to testify to, and at times to lovingly witness against, the stiff-necked generation he finds himself in. For God makes no mistakes! He places His servants where they need to be to bring Him the glory He deserves. Even though Moses was slow of speech and tongue, haven't his words reverberated throughout history?

But as our Lord told our cousin Nicodemus, though the Light has come into the world, men loved the Darkness instead because their deeds were evil. For light exposes the deeds of darkness. So the men who love evil will do everything in their power to extinguish the light, lest they be exposed.

Stephen's life demonstrates this reality for your pilgrim. For after Stephen testified to the truth, what did the Jews do to him? Did they not cover their ears, yell at the top of their voices, and rush at Stephen with hands full of stones? Did they not kill the Lord's servant at the feet of Saul? They sought to snuff out the light of Stephen's testimony.

But though Stephen sacrificed his mortal life for the gospel, the Light living within him was not extinguished! Stephen looked up and saw the glory of Heaven and the Son of Man standing at the right hand of our Father. And the faithful witness, Stephen, then passed into the Presence of our Lord. But not before his testimony planted God's seed in the heart of Saul—the man poised to become Christ's mouthpiece to the world.

As you no doubt recall, Barnabas, Stephen's death became God's seed for the gospel's growth. For unless a seed falls to the ground, it cannot bear fruit. Saul would never forget what he witnessed in Stephen's death. The Spirit planted His seed. For the rest of his earthly life, Saul (one day Paul) would count himself as the "worst of sinners" for his participation in the martyr's death. And the Lord, who would one day meet Saul on the Damascus road, would redeem

Stephen's sacrifice in the heart of Saul for the glory of His Holy Name.

With these thoughts in mind, dear Barnabas, plumb the resolve of your pilgrim. Through the Spirit, test his heart and mind to see if there is any offensive way in him. Is he ready to testify for Christ before the angry mob? Is he willing to give his life for the gospel?

Until you are confident, my brother, your man is fully equipped for these challenges, persist in your work. Attend to the details we have described. And through the grace and glory of the God who revealed Himself to Stephen, I am confident that even your man might become a light in the darkness that the powers of the Darkness cannot extinguish!

Affectionately yours,
## Uriel

# Letter 29

*Beloved Barnabas,*

*Based on the prayers your pilgrim has recently offered, your careful probing of his commitment is bearing fruit. I'm convinced he now more fully understands the true demands of Love's call. So let us be faithful to assist him in the fulfillment!*

*With this as our objective, my most recent communication made reference to Saul of Tarsus and his participation in the stoning of Stephen. Because of this grim beginning, the life of Saul—transformed into the Paul we know and love well—has an enormous amount to teach students of faith like your pilgrim. For few lives have been more mightily used by the Spirit to instruct and exhort the pilgrims' progress than Paul's.*

*But the Paul who carried the gospel to the edges of the known world was formerly Saul, the persecutor of the Church. And the story of faith Paul has to tell, depends entirely upon the Saul who preceded it. Here's what I mean....*

*Paul's life of faith on earth was marked by a conviction in two things: the depth of his own sinfulness and the enormity of God's love and grace as manifested in Christ Jesus. As Paul's letters reveal, these two truths are foundational requirements for a healthy spiritual life. No one* will reach the Kingdom without embracing both axioms.

As you employ Paul's witness in the fine tuning of your pilgrim's heart, dear Barnabas, first root your efforts in the Apostle's resolute self-awareness of his own sinfulness. Perhaps because Saul's heart was such an open enemy of Christ, the transformed Paul never forgot the depth of his sin. Indeed, as Paul told our cousin Timothy, the Apostle considered himself the "worst of sinners."

Now on this point your pilgrim may object: How can the champion of faith, the Apostle Paul, be the "worst of sinners"? Isn't this righteous hyperbole? What about the executive who brazenly embezzles employee retirement funds, the wife who repeatedly cheats on her husband, or that crazed dictator who slaughtered millions of his own countrymen? Are they not more sinful than Paul? Objection noted. But of course, you must remind your man: sin is sin. There is no escape in a sliding scale. All men are guilty.

At the same time, however, don't fail to use this line of questioning to your advantage, Barnabas. For make sure to point out that the closer a man's heart is to Christ's, the more fully he becomes aware of his own sinfulness and hypocrisy. Conversely, our enemy knows that the man who is most blind is the one who believes himself "better than most." The devil will constantly play his trump card of comparison to keep a man from facing the truth of himself. But because Paul's heart was so close to Christ, he was not duped. His plumb line was never another man, however sinful, but the Son of man. And as a result, he was always vitally aware of just how much sin remained in his life! Paul was, as all men are, an inveterate sinner on earth. The only difference was, he knew it!

Indeed, in his letter to the Romans, Paul divulges a keen awareness of his propensity to sin. He goes so far as to count himself a slave to sin. For what he wanted to do he did not do. Instead, he found himself doing what he hated, for sin lived in him. Paul's spirit was never far from the constant war waged by his sinful nature. He recognized evil was right there with him.

In light of Paul's example, impress upon your man the depth of his own sinfulness. Take whatever means necessary, Barnabas, to remind him that his sins are like the hairs on his head—uncountable. Further still, how the battle for his beleaguered soul is waged one decision at a time. For though your pilgrim has given himself to Christ, our enemy will not stop his pursuit while any breath remains in your man! The race is not over till it's over. And while Christ has defeated sin on the cross, sin dies a slow, lingering death in the hearts of men.

This grim knowledge of his own sinfulness, however, must be carefully counterweighted with the glorious hope of salvation. For otherwise, a man like your pilgrim will succumb to despair and we will lose his heart to the enemy. The letters Paul left stress this essential balance.

In fact, no sooner did Paul despair at his own proclivity for sin, than he rejoiced in the rescue he obtained from death through the work of Jesus Christ our Lord! From the moment Paul was rescued on the Damascus road, he was never far from Heaven's hope. Paul recognized his salvation was by grace, not by works he could boast in, but a priceless gift. The knowledge of this gift, and the love that bestowed it upon him, energized his entire ministry.

In like manner, your man's awareness of his own sin must be met with the constant reminder of the grace he has received in Christ. When your pilgrim despairs of his sinfulness, bring him back to the hope Scripture declares. If our enemy causes your charge to question his salvation (or worse yet, the love behind it!), then focus his eyes on Paul's conviction that nothing—death, life, present, future, height nor depth—can separate him from the love of God that is in Christ Jesus!

If our Lord permits the devil to hound your pilgrim's life, point your man's attention to Paul's testimony: Though hard pressed on every side, he was not crushed; though perplexed, he did not succumb to despair; though persecuted, he was not abandoned by the Spirit; though struck down, he was not destroyed. For Paul lived with the conviction that his light and momentary troubles were achieving for him an eternal glory that far outweighs any earthly prize.

Using this approach, dear Barnabas, I am confident you will continue to guard, guide and grace the life of your pilgrim under your careful supervision. With Paul's example, you will both encourage and challenge your pilgrim at the same time. As you do, the spirit will work through you to give your man the hope of glory. And one day he too will join this great cloud of witnesses!

Affectionately yours,

Uriel

# Letter 30

Beloved Barnabas,

I am pleased, but in no way surprised, that our recent exploration of Paul's conviction in faith has struck a chord in your man's heart. For what little I know of your pilgrim from this distance, he is clearly a man of conviction. The trick is channeling that conviction in the right direction. For the world is full of convictions, some of them more laudable than others.

But this much is true of all the competing causes: they are eternally meaningless without Christ. He is the Author and Perfecter of faith. As a result, any attempt to remove His agency from the world's narratives leaves nothing but a doomed jumble of nonsensical words and futile efforts—no matter how strong the convictions, good the intentions, or noble the causes. What's more, there are no words themselves, much less a story, without Christ. For He is the Word. He is the beginning and ending of all things!

On this note, it is not only fitting, but necessary, for us to wrap up our examination of faith with our Lord Christ Himself. For that is exactly where the letter to the Hebrews leads us. After alluding to the great cloud of witnesses we have recently discussed, the Spirit exhorts the pilgrim to throw off the sin that so easily entangles and to run with perseverance the race set before him. But not just to run aimlessly, or even for the sake of running itself. But to run with purpose! This pilgrim of yours is called to press on toward the goal; to fix his eyes on Jesus, the Author and Perfecter of faith; and to never, never, never give up!

Of course, as the Author of all things, Christ knows your pilgrim's beginning and his end. All the days ordained for your man were written in Christ's book before your charge ever drew a feeble breath. To underscore this point, do not fail to draw your pilgrim's attention to the beloved Apostle's record: "In the beginning was the Word, and the Word was with God, and the Word was God." Christ was with God in the beginning, before our angelic host was created, much less the men we have been charged to guard and guide. And through Christ our Lord, all things were made. Nothing that was, or is, or ever will be, exists apart from Him. He is the Author of all things.

To be sure, this is no news to you, my brother. But I stress it now for the sake of your pilgrim. Make sure he reflects on the fact that as the Author, Christ might have written a simple fairytale devoid of conflict, sorrow or suffering. But He didn't. And He didn't for a reason. For what love comes without choice and the potential for conflict? What beauty or strength without

191

toil and suffering?    Our Lord might have remained solely the disengaged Author (as if this were nothing in and of itself!) and not also a character in the story He wrote. But he couldn't help getting involved. For in giving freedom to men, He allowed for the Fall. But in the falling, He made way for redemption. He chose to enter His story so the faithful might find the fulfillment of their faith!

This was the joy set before Him, that He chose to subject Himself to men.    He stooped down to make them great, enduring the cross and scorning its shame. I know you cringed alongside me, Barnabas, when those vile men whipped our Lord's mortal flesh and crowned Him with thorns; when they plunged the spear into His side, and hurled their insolent jests at their Maker. How gently and humbly He bore it all!

But I swear, if our Lord did not raise His hand in restraint, Michael would have destroyed those infidels in an instant. I almost wished he would have.    It would have spared us a lot of heartbreaking work! And Michael's wings were literally itching to do it. What torture for the General to stand by and do nothing!

But such was, and is, the love of Christ for men, that He willingly lay down His life before those barbarous cretins. He could have called ten thousand legions of angels to His rescue, but He didn't. And because He didn't, never let your pilgrim forget Christ's sacrifice, dear Barnabas. Sear it on his brain; write it on the back of his hand if you must, but do not let him neglect what Christ has done for him.

More than this, however, set forth Christ, the Author of faith, as the ultimate exemplar of faith. For though we have exposed your pilgrim to the faith of many devout pilgrims in the cloud of witnesses, all of their faith is but a flawed trifle compared to Christ's. His faith set the example for the holy fear and humility our King desires.

You remember it, of course: How our Lord knelt in the Garden of Gethsemane and prayed tears of blood; how the heart of the Son of God wrestled with the flesh of the Son of Man. It was agony to watch! But in the end, Christ's faith in the Father prevailed. He taught us all—"Not my will, but yours, O Lord, be done."

This is the essence of faith for your pilgrim, Barnabas—the life that lays itself down because it is convinced God is who He says He is: the great, I AM! When your pilgrim finally reaches this epiphany, nothing, not even the agony of the cross, will impede his divine calling.

But total acquiescence does not come easily. And so our Lord is not only the Author and exemplar of faith, but also its Perfecter. He knows your pilgrim inside and out, and He will take all measures to make your man perfect. For has He not said, "Be perfect, therefore, as your heavenly Father is perfect"? So Christ disciplines your man as a father would a son. He allows pain, suffering and tribulation to enter your pilgrim's journey to refine his heart into pure gold. And of course, our Lord has placed us in your man's life as well, to guide, guard and protect him; to ensure he is not tempted beyond what he can handle, nor tortured by the enemy more than Christ would allow for His glory and your man's good.

What a privilege it is to serve this King! What an honor to be one of His servants. Knowing this, make every effort, my dear brother, to reveal this truth to your pilgrim as well. Help foster in him a deep-seated desire—a longing that no words can express—to emulate our service and join in the company of the cloud of witnesses. For then your pilgrim will be with Him, our Lord and Savior. He will see Him face to face. And in that radiance, your pilgrim's faith will finally make sense. Every sacrifice he has made, every trial he has endured, and every loss he has absorbed, will be as nothing compared to the surpassing greatness of knowing Jesus Christ our Lord!

In the hope of this glory, I leave you to the finishing touches!

Affectionately yours,
## Uriel

# Acknowledgements

I am so very thankful for all those friends, family members, and saints of the faith—that great cloud of witnesses, past and present—who have supported my pilgrimage so far. Their prayers, counsel, companionship and examples have been the instruments of God's grace in my life. I am also indebted to my brother in Christ, C.S. Lewis, whose spiritual wisdom and intellectual rigor have been guiding lights in my journey of faith from childhood onward. Specifically, Professor Lewis' *The Screwtape Letters* helped inspire this book. And whether this current work hits the target Lewis alluded to or not, I am grateful for the Spirit's inspiration through the professor's work. If nothing else, I hope this book glorifies the King, Christ my Lord and His angelic host—the Love that surrounds me, and the hands that faithfully guide and guard me.

# ABOUT THE AUTHOR

Dr. Eubanks is blessed to be a pilgrim making progress on his journey home. On the way, his mission field is currently medicine, where he serves an Associate Professor of Orthopaedic Surgery at Case Western Reserve University School of Medicine and the Chief and Director of Spine Surgery at University Hospitals Ahuja Medical Center. He is the author of numerous books, including: *Book of Hours: Meditations for the Heart after God* and *More of Him, Less of Me: A Doctor's Devotional for Spiritual Health*. He has written over 20 peer-reviewed scientific publications, multiple textbook chapters and editorials, and poetry appearing in journals such as *JAMA*, *The Annals of Internal Medicine*, *Tar River Poetry*, and more. He lives outside of Cleveland, Ohio.

**Author page:**

https://www.amazon.com/stores/Jason-David-Eubanks-MD/author/B08D8MGW53

www.ingramcontent.com/pod-product-compliance
Lightning Source LLC
LaVergne TN
LVHW051257080426
835509LV00020B/3025